THE PARENTAL VOICE

About the Editors

Robert Holzberg, Ed.D. is Professor Emeritus at Chicago State University, Chicago, Illinois, and Adjunct Professor of Psychology, Wolfson Campus, Miami Dade Community College, Miami, Florida. His earlier positions in the field include teacher, supervisor of programs for the multiply handicapped for the state of South Carolina, principal, and teacher-educator. Dr. Holzberg is a member of Council for Exceptional Children. He is also a family arbitrator for the state of Florida.

Sara Walsh-Burton, M.Ed. has an equally long history in the field of special education, specializing in the education of the deaf-blind. She has served as a classroom teacher, program evaluator, personnel development specialist, and consultant. Currently she is an independent consultant working with the severely handicapped.

THE PARENTAL VOICE

Problems Faced by Parents of the Deaf-Blind, Severely and Profoundly Handicapped Child

Edited by

ROBERT HOLZBERG, Ed.D.

and

SARA WALSH-BURTON, M.Ed.

CHARLES C THOMAS • PUBLISHER
Springfield • Illinois • U.S.A.

Published and Distributed Throughout the World by

CHARLES C THOMAS • PUBLISHER
2600 South First Street
Springfield, Illinois 62794-9265

©*1996 by* CHARLES C THOMAS • PUBLISHER
ISBN 0-398-06553-5   (cloth)
ISBN 0-398-06554-3   (paper)
Library of Congress Catalog Card Number: 95-30790

Printed in the United States of America
SC-R-3

Library of Congress Cataloging-in-Publication Data

The parental voice : problems faced by parents of the deaf-blind, severely
and profoundly handicapped child, edited by Robert Holzberg and Sara
Walsh-Burton.
    p.   cm.
  ISBN 0-398-06553-5 (cloth). — ISBN 0-398-06554-3 (paper)
  1. Parents of handicapped children—Psychology.   2. Parents of
handicapped children—Attitudes.   3. Parents of handicapped
children—Family relationships.   I. Holzberg, Robert.   II. Walsh-
Burton, Sara.
HQ759.913.H69   1995
649'.151—dc20
                                             95-30790
                                              CIP

CONTRIBUTORS

ALAN BALTER, Ph.D.
Professor
Chicago State University
Chicago, Illinois

PAUL D. COTTON, Ph.D.
Director
Boswell Retardation Center
Sanatorium, Mississippi

HARRY L. DANGEL
Associate Professor
Department of Special Education
University of Georgia
Athens, Georgia

GEORGIA GRANBERRY
Program Coordinator
Residential Deaf Blind Program
Ellisville State School Retardation Center
Ellisville, Mississippi

ROBERT HOLZBERG, Ed.D.
Professor Emeritus
Chicago State University
Chicago, Illinois

WAYNE LASHER
Associate Psychologist
Pecan Grove ICR
Ellisville, Mississippi

KEVIN D. MAGIN
Consultant
Michigan Department of Education
Lansing, Michigan

PEARL E. TAIT
Florida State University
Tallahassee, Florida

v

SARA WALSH–BURTON, M.Ed.
Consultant
Talladega, Alabama

MARYANNE B. WARD
Special Education Consultant
Tallahassee, Florida

This book is dedicated to all parents of Deaf-Blind children and youth worldwide. In an effort to rear and educate their children they have suffered heartbreak, bewilderment, and extreme frustration; however, they have been strong of will and mind in their endeavor to get just the basic education (to the potential) of their children.

They have been given a responsibility so great it is difficult for others to grasp. For their efforts they deserve much recognition. We recognize them and dedicate this book to them for all they have and continue to endure.

PREFACE

Dear reader, you are about to read a work in special education. It is not, however, organized like the usual text with which you may be familiar. This is a book essentially written by parents who will tell you about the problems which they have faced in parenting a child with severe and/or profound handicaps.

All of our work in special education has been focused upon the child, his developmental status, his psychological needs, and the methodologies required to educate and develop those skills of independent living to the greatest degree possible. While the emphasis upon the child is certainly required, in all the effort expended, parents have received very little attention.

Very little has been written concerning the effect of severe and/or profound handicap not only upon the child, but upon the parents. What happens to parents when their child for whom they waited for almost a year and who represents their hopes and dreams for the future is born with a severe handicap or such a handicap develops soon after birth? What is the effect upon the marriage?, upon the other children in the family? How do parents deal with the severe emotional, social, and monetary problems presented? How do they find needed services? What happens when services are far away or are not even available? How does the handicap change parents and their attitudes toward their own child, towards the medical profession, and toward governmental authorities? This book attempts to answer these questions and give you a better understanding of the coping process in action. The questions are answered through the voices of the parents themselves. Parents from differing backgrounds and cultures have written their stories. After each story in section one, you will find an interpretation and commentary by an authority in the field. The distinctive nature of this work is that it is not, like the usual text in special education, written about a problem or set of problems. Here the parents themselves reveal to you their inner-most feelings, doubts, fears, angers, frustrations, hopes, and joys.

The purpose of this work is not to draw a particular conclusion. It is rather to give you a view into the lives of a group of parents who have had to deal with some of the most difficult emotional, social and economic problems faced by any group of parents and how they found the inner resources to cope.

R.H.
S.W.B.

ABOUT THE BOOK

Just as our first book, UNDERSTANDING AND EDUCATING THE DEAF–BLIND, SEVERELY AND PROFOUNDLY HANDICAPPED— An International Perspective, this book found its seed at the Southeast Regional Center for the Deaf-Blind. I served at this Center for eleven years as Personnel Development Specialist. During those years I was responsible for the printing of a newsletter that served our educators and parents, both nationally and internationally. It was through this newsletter that I urged parents of Deaf-Blind children to share their experiences with us. The response was quick and gratifying.

The stories in this book are products of that request. Their submission was voluntary and with the understanding that the stories would be drawn together as a book for the edification of parents, educators, and others who work with the Deaf-Blind. You will note several are from foreign countries. It was our intent to retain the international perspective.

It is our hope that parents of deaf-blind children and youth and other handicapped children everywhere will read this book of "blood and tears" stories and use it for the knowledge it provides and be soothed in spirit by the feelings so expressly portrayed by fellow sufferers.

S.W.B.

ABOUT THE PROFESSIONAL CONTRIBUTORS

All those professionals contributing to this book have done so voluntarily. Their works have been given to increase the body of knowledge of the field of Deaf-Blind Education and to offer parents, educators, and significant others in the field experiences and knowledge they have gained in their own work with this special population of children and youth.

It is with sincere thanks and admiration that we acknowledge all these contributors.

R.H.
S.W.B.

ACKNOWLEDGMENTS

A WORD OF THANKS TO THE PARENTS
WHO AUTHORED OUR STORIES

What you have done is a very hard thing. To think back over the years, about the handicaps which your child has experienced and the effects which those handicaps have had upon your child and upon the total family, and the steps which you took to help the child and the total family has not been easy. Hopefully, your experience will help other parents to deal with those developmental problems which they face. Please accept our heartfelt thanks for your efforts.

R.H.
S.W.B.

CONTENTS

THE PARENTAL VOICE

Section One

STORIES WITH
PSYCHOLOGICAL INTERPRETATION

CARA

This is Cara's story and I am Cara's mother, Cherry. Besides being a homemaker, I am an interpreter/tutor for a deaf child who attends a regular hearing school. Let me introduce our family: Chuck is father and a high-school librarian. Our oldest daughter is Jo, who is 18 years old and a grade 13 student. For three summers Jo has been a summer intervenor with a deaf-blind teenager, hard work when you come home to a demanding sister who is also deaf-blind. Cara is 12 years old—a very special daughter about whom this love story is written in the hope that it may help other families realize that they are not "alone." Our son, Todd, is 11 years old, in grade 6, and a support and model for Cara who is just one year older.

As I have been writing Cara's story, I feel joy and thankfulness that we have made it this far, still intact. Life now is comparatively "easy." (Perhaps there is a better word, I am at a loss to find it.) Cara is multisensory deprived. I don't think I need explain how varied this handicap can be from individual to individual. Cara is using her limited vision extremely well, but she has a profound hearing loss. She has boundless energy and is not a child to withdraw or sit placidly waiting to be motivated. In the past, this resulted in a great deal of frustration for her and for us. However, because of her development and the gains she has made, there is much less stress surrounding her care. When Cara is away at school we do things any family would. It is often a time to try-out and test experiences in which we may want to involve Cara in the future. More often it is an opportunity to relax after carrying out our individual routines. When Cara is home, we involve her totally. Her energy usually outlasts all others. Cara relaxes by pouring through books, catalogues, and playing with toys (Barbies and cars).

Cara was born in Fredericton, New Brunswick in June, 1970. Many times I have been asked about problems encountered during that pregnancy. In 1969–70, I was teaching school and so was exposed to many possible viruses. I recall missing only one day of classes due to a very sore throat; that was in mid-January. Visits to the doctor were usually encouraging. (I asked him about flouride tablets because I was concerned about the baby having strong teeth, this seems too insignificant now.) For a week or so in each of the sixth and seventh months, I took phenobarb for high blood pressure. I remember those last few months with a feeling of complete tiredness and I did very little other than my school preparations and getting through the day in class. Thank heaven for a liberated husband who did more than his share. I had a week at home before Cara was born on June 8th. We went back to school the last week of June to finish report cards and the paperwork. Cara slept contentedly in her basket by my desk.

Cara's delivery was easy. We drove into the city to the hospital at about 11:00 P.M. and she was born at 1:30 A.M. I remember not needing any anesthesia and required no stitches. Cara weighed 7 pounds 1 ounce. It was a happy peaceful time with lots of family around. As much as is possible with a new baby, things went well at home. Cara ate and slept well. She hated bathtimes those first few weeks. She really liked to be cuddled and would hold on tight; especially to my hair which was long then.

On the July 1st holiday, Cara was three weeks old and we were driving 125 miles to our hometown to show-off the "new baby." On the morning we were due to leave, Cara awoke with a red rash. It covered her body and she felt warm, I called the local clinic. The doctor (whom I didn't know) asked me about formula. I told him she was on Enfalac® and because she seemed so hungry I had given her some thin pablum. Right away, he said the rash was food allergy and he did a great job of making this mother feel terribly guilty and stupid! (I've wondered about that rash many times over the past years.) We made the trip, but I was still worried and phoned another doctor in my hometown who admitted he had no idea what it was but he gave us some soothing ointment. It wasn't a very "pretty baby" we had to show-off. By the time we returned home, two or three days later, the rash had gone and Cara's skin started to peel. I took her to my doctor who was anxious to see us both. He explained that it was not unusual for newborns to "peel." I was also concerned about a "strawberry birthmark" on her head. That would go away.

The remaining summer was pleasant. Cara slept outside in her carriage most afternoons. We were preparing to move to Labrador where Chuck had a new teaching position and Jo would start school.

Cara was three months old when we settled in Wabush, Labrador.

Other than a bit of five o'clock cholic she was doing well. She was happy and chubby.

On December 4, 1970, "the day the world crashed in around us," I had taken Jo to the doctor with a throat infection. While we were with the doctor I asked him to look at Cara's left eye; it seemed to be turning inward. Over the previous few weeks, Cara was spending most of her waking hours looking at her fists, hands, fingers. The doctor looked at Cara, tried to get her to sit alone (which she almost did and was doing three days later). Then he said to me, "Mother, you must know that your baby is mentally deficient." Even now, eleven years later, this is so vivid to me that the physical pain of that heartbreak comes back with the memory.

Painful as that time was, our family is blessed with a father who is the eternal optimist. Beginning then, and through the next five years of looking for an appropriate diagnosis, Chuck would say, "I don't know that (. . . regarding a certain professional opinion) but I do know Cara." Thankfully, Cara herself gave us many encouraging signs when we needed them most.

New Year 1971 began in the fear of "not knowing." I refused to take Cara back to the clinic. We made contacts with the family doctors back home in Moncton, New Brunswick. The appointments were set for the Easter holiday, and we flew home for that. Those three and a half months are an absolute blur. By mid-January, I realized that I was pregnant again. Cara had learned to use her walker and was pulling herself up on her feet. Our family drew strength from close friends who were thoughtful, loving, and very supportive. The warmth of that small community gave us much needed encouragement.

April 1971 was the beginning of the many, many medical assessments Cara was to undergo. The first was with Dr. B., the ophthalmologist, who saw the cataracts in the early stages. He questioned whether we suspected a hearing loss. No, we hadn't! He explained fully what we could expect from the cataracts and how they would be removed. Nothing should be done at that time. The next day we saw Dr. L., a pediatrician. He spent a great deal of time with the three of us, Chuck, Cara, and me. His concerns were with large muscle development. He measured her head and ordered a skull X-ray. He also questioned us regarding a loss of hearing. He wanted us to take Cara to the Isaac Walton Killam Hospital in Halifax for a complete assessment. In June, we travelled to Halifax; Cara was admitted into the children's hospital. We met Dr. T., the neurologist, who explained the barage of tests he would do. The medical team included specialists in neurology, ophthalmology, E.N.T., and pediatrics. This was one of the ultimate "lows" for us. Being separated as a family, Cara was frightened at being in the hospital, and I was six weeks away from delivering Todd. My fears for Cara were multiplied by my fears for this new baby. Chuck and I slept in a rooming house near the hospital so we could be there quickly should Cara need us. While in the hospital, Cara developed an infection and it was three and a half weeks before she came home. The diagnosis was that Cara was physically doing things appropriate to her age "norm." There was little or no hearing loss, but some sort of latent-language development. What I remember about the rubella tests was that someone came to Cara's room early one morning and took blood samples from Cara and me. Later that day we got the message that there were no rubella toxoids in either blood test. As Cara came home, we had positive feelings from the doctor. She should be stimulated and included in all of our family activities. Our love and encouragement were all she needed at this time. He wanted to see her again the next year. I was puzzled that he felt it necessary to say that. Didn't everyone give these things to all their children? Cara learned to walk at fourteen months. This was how she greeted Todd and I when we came home from the hospital.

We spent the next three years in Labrador. We flew to the specialists' appointments at regular intervals. Our local clinic acquired three young doctors who were a pleasant change and who gave us reassurance again and again. Cara developed some seizure activity at two and a half years. This frightened us a great deal, but the doctors' explanations eased our worries. Cara was given a mild dosage of Dilantin, and there were no problems for the next few years.

At two and a half Cara's left eye was turned in and clouded white. In the summer of her third year, she had the cataract removed and six months later had more surgery to straighten that eye. The doctor did an excellent job and it was heartening to look into those big brown eyes which were now clear and straight. Cara coped so well visually that I had to remind myself of the extent of her visual impairment. She had the most difficulty on the bright wintry days, which were numerous in Labrador.

We were constantly "testing" to find out if she could hear; banging pots, calling her name, popping balloons, dropping things—loud noises and soft sounds. We just became confused!

It was a frustrating time. Cara wasn't sleeping at nights. Some days she just cried all day. More nerve-wracking were the days when she laughed all day—running and giggling. We tried various medications to calm her: Ritalin—no reaction, Valium made her hyper, Benylin gave us two or three nights sleep but after that, no difference; even children's aspirin seemed to make her hyper. Our best "friend" was an old rocking chair.

The doctor's assessments continued throughout those years. Nothing seemed to be "the answer."

By the time Cara was four we decided to leave Labrador to find an appropriate educational setting for her. Chuck resigned his teaching position. We decided on London, Ontario. He wrote dozens of applications to London and surrounding areas. When we arrived in town all he had was a job interview with an insurance company. This was another low point in our morale and just the beginning to finding a suitable education for Cara. Having left the comfort of our small close-knit community, we were lost in the big city without family or friends. We began immediately with a new pediatrician, new ophthalmologist, audiologist, and psychologist. The audiologist could not get a successful audiogram. All the psychological testing just seemed to upset Cara. The ophthalmologist kept close watch on the right eye which required several appointments.

More periods of not sleeping, hours of crying, and fussing. During the first four months in London, along with the medical assessments, we began our search for an appropriate educational setting. Three nursery schools were considered. One was especially designed for physically disabled, mentally retarded children; the second was for low functioning mentally retarded children; and the third was a nursery which dealt with behavior problems and learning disabled. By November, it was decided Cara would attend the third, Madam Vaniers Childrens' Center; Cara certainly was a behavior problem. The teacher, Mrs. H., was wonderful.

When Cara started Madam Vanier's Nursery, she had no structured language. She was 4½ years old. A few months later, our new pediatrician, Dr. S., suggested that we take a total communication class at the local community college. "Total Communication" meant nothing to us. I thought it would help Cara understand what we were saying. Probably, we would learn to be more expressive and to use body language. Looking back on the many many professional opinions we had received, I wonder why no one told us about "total communication." Most of Cara's frustration was due to the lack of language. Why we didn't consider "sign language" ourselves, I don't know. Until this time, we did not know a deaf person. The total communication class was a ten-week introductory course. We continued with TC classes for two years. The first lessons were frightening, because of our lack of ability to sign and even less understanding of the signs given to us by deaf persons. It was our first contact with deaf adults. The fear and nervousness that those first confrontations created were a worthwhile lesson. For some time we were the noncommunicative minority. It gave us a lot of insight into the isolation that this disability creates.

In time we became more involved in the local association for the deaf. Our involvement often included Cara and we noticed immediately how she responded to deaf friends. We are so grateful to them for their patience in helping us understand the handicap and feel comfortable with it. The first word Cara understood was "apple." If I signed "apple," she would point to the fruit basket on the kitchen counter.

On the school scene, Cara's behavior improved gradually. She loved school. They worked on increasing her attention span at quiet activities. Sitting at the table for meals was always a problem. Mrs. H. spent much time working on that. Todd was a big help in those days because Cara would follow his model and she always was more relaxed when Todd was included in activities at school, speech therapy, or any of the psychological testing that was going on. Throughout this year Cara was having speech therapy two afternoons a week. It was very discouraging; after months of work at the therapist's office and at home, we could get Cara to make only a few sounds. These sounds she made convinced the therapist that Cara had a profound hearing loss. We questioned whether it was worthwhile to continue these sessions at this time. This was also the year that the second cataract clouded her right eye. Surgery was scheduled for the summer.

In the spring, just before Cara's fifth birthday, we asked the Robarts School for the Hearing Impaired to do an educational assessment. We felt so fortunate that the superintendent himself would do the assessing. Surely this professional with all his expertise would recognize Cara's disability and set her and us on the right road. It had been a long time coming, but we felt certain there would be a total communication kindergarten where Cara's needs would be met. Our hopes were dashed again! First of all, the school did not have a total communication kindergarten. Second, the communication policy was Visible English (finger-spelling). Cara didn't see well enough for that. "But," I explained, "Cara is beginning to understand some 'signing'." The school didn't encourage 'signing,' but if that was all she could do. . . . Two points were strongly impressed: one, that it is very rare that a deaf-blind person is not severely retarded as well; and two, there was a deaf-blind unit at the school for the blind in Brantford. Perhaps we should see them. Another all time low! Chuck and I talked this one out for hours and days. I think it is important to know that Cara still had days of whining, crying, giggling, running, and I was very concerned about her emotional health. She was also quite small for her age and the mere idea of sending her away to school was beyond consideration. The teachers at nursery school were a support, they respected our feelings. They realized how much happiness and comfort Cara gained from home and family. They agreed to keep her another year. We still had hopes that once Cara had the cataract removed and was wearing corrective lens, she might fit into classes for the deaf.

Cara had the surgery in August. The operation and postoperative care went very well. The ophthalmologist was encouraging. By October we had glasses. The doctor prepared us for this slow process. A new professional entered Cara's world. The optometrist, Dr. E., had a great deal of experience with children, and he was constantly reassuring us. His patience with Cara was remarkable. She was prepared for a fight every time we went near the office. It took weeks and months to get her used to the glasses. In the beginning, a good day was getting Cara to keep her glasses on for fifteen minutes. It was a family chore to hold Cara, hold her head, her hands, and turn the pages of an interesting picture book! Once she was wearing them continually, I was frequently surprised to find that she would come in from outdoor play without her glasses. On different occasions she buried them in the sand box, dumped them on a neighbor's lawn, or just left them laying about the yard. Dr. E. was constantly repairing the damage.

Cara's fifth year. Madame Vanier's nursery school continued to be a strength and support. Cara's behavior was much more controlled, but one of the major problems now was her independence. She wanted to explore and often would sneak away to the parking lot, the cafeteria, or play area designated for older children. Mrs. H. found the best way to communicate was with drawings. We still have those notebooks of stick-men, named Cara, doing good and bad things. Cara will still get upset when looking at those old pictures that have a red X and a "no-no" written on them.

Another new person entered Cara's life. We were given a home-visiting teacher from the school for the deaf. V. was a very good teacher and had many excellent ideas and aids, some of which I still use. Cara loved these visits, especially the new toys she found in V's tote bag. These visits were usually enjoyable and gave me encouraging support; however, Canadian winters—road conditions and illnesses caused these sessions to be quite sporadic.

This was a winter when Cara had constant colds, runney nose, sore throats, ear infections. The doctor attempted a myrengotimes, but could never get Cara a hospital bed when she didn't have an upper respiratory infection. I might add here that any dental work Cara had done had to be done under anesthetic because she would not tolerate a dentist. Hospital experiences were dreadful.

This year, we also decided that Cara needed input in regular school setting. We enrolled her at a Montessori Nursery School two afternoons per week. She enjoyed the sensory activities, spent many concentrated periods working at puzzles, and in general picked up good habits from the children around her.

Now that Cara was wearing her glasses, and her behavior had improved, we asked for another assessment by the Robarts school. It is with pain and a clammy-fear that I recall that testing session. Cara was age 5½. The tests were done at the school for the deaf by the superintendent and a psychologist. Cara, her teacher, and I drove to the appointment. We were ushered into the room . . . the table was too high for Cara to sit at . . . it was flipped over—legs shortened to a suitable height. A startled Cara had no time to acquaint herself with that room, the new people, or the materials. Abruptly she was directed to make a line with a black marker—she refused. She was given three red blocks to pile—she refused, I was so upset that I left the room saying to myself "Cara you are tougher than I am, stick it out!" I paced the waiting room and decided that Cara would be better off at home. I'd teach her myself, somehow. I knew if she were accepted at this school, she would just be a big problem. I felt there was no love or warmth or respect for Cara here. That would be priority if I ever found a school; until then, I would keep her home. When the man came out of the assessment room, he explained to me that Cara was severely retarded, and functionally was a two or three year old. Since I had already made up my mind on this facility and Cara's education, I was not upset with what this Ph.D. in Psychology had to say. My only regret was putting Cara through the past hour and thinking this man's file on Cara will probably haunt us forever! Oh well! I really felt better about things than I had in months.

Cara continued at Madame Vanier's. She seemed to be understanding some of our signs, but so far she hadn't made any signs of her own.

Enter another professional on the scene. Coincidentally, a child psychologist, Mrs. P., from the Canadian National Institute for the Blind visited Cara's nursery to see another partially-sighted child. Mrs. H., a teacher, asked her to observe Cara. Cara was piling blocks! If I remember correctly, they were 17 blocks high so that Cara had to stand on a chair to reach the top. Mrs. P. read the dreaded assessment on Cara. She phoned me to say she felt the assessment on Cara was totally off base. In her opinion, Cara was multisensory deprived. I wanted to scream at her and tell her to leave us alone. I know I was very rude, but she was persistent. Mrs. P. was the twenty-eighth "professional" to enter our lives via Cara. She said she knew other children much like Cara, and she wanted us to meet them. Since I had made the decision that Cara would be educated at home, my fears and intimidations were under control. Now I was just plain angry! The first few visits Mrs. P. made to our home must have been frustrating for her. I didn't want to hear any more. I closed my ears totally to her words. She kept it up and even arranged for Cara, Todd, and I to visit a family who lived nearby. Their daughter, who was then eleven, was multisensory deprived. Mrs. P. was partially sighted herself, but she had her driver pick us up one day and we drove to visit the L. family. It was Tuesday following Easter; T. L. was home and getting ready to go back to school in Brantford that evening. T. L. was the first child I met who even resembled Cara in her disability. Mrs. L. told us about J. M. and J. T. who coordinated the deaf-blind program at the W. R. MacDonald School in Brantford. Mrs. L. told me I would be so lucky if Cara was accepted! The deaf-blind unit was reported to be wonderful. T. L. loved school. She was making great progress there. Mrs. P. arranged for the coordinators of the program to visit Cara at her nursery school. She talked about the importance of observing and assessing Cara in a setting where she was comfortable. How sensible! I believe it was April of that year that they saw Cara in the nursery school. Later that day, they came to our home. I remember Cara running to them with her arms up. I couldn't believe it. Cara was always so shy, especially with men. Cara's reaction to these two people surprised me so that I really cannot remember much of our conversation. I know they invited us to visit their school. They felt Cara would definitely be a candidate for their program. There was no pressure. If we could find an appropriate facility in London they would serve as resource persons.

Cara, Mrs. H., another teacher from Madame Vanier's, and I drove to Brantford to the W. R. MacDonald School. We were welcomed at the front door by the superintendent, John, and Jacquie. They took us through the school. In the gross-motor room Jacquie made a videotape of Cara riding a bike and playing on the equipment. Cara had a wonderful day. When we left, Cara was screaming and clutching the door jamb, and I was dragging her to the car. At home, I tried to explain everything I saw to Chuck. We decided to go again. A few weeks later, two very good friends, Chuck, Cara, and I made a return visit. Unlike the first reports I had heard, I found the children busy at challenging endeavors. Living skills were strongly emphasized. Language took many forms. Total communication was encouraged, for the children and their families. Now Chuck and I were really agonizing. If I were looking for love, warmth, and respect, this place had it.

We filled out the application forms and decided if Cara was accepted, we would send her to this program for the multisensory deprived.

Cara was six years old. We left Madame Vanier's, with gratitude to the many friends who helped Cara and so helped us.

We attended a week long summer school for Parents of Pre-school Deaf Children at the Robarts School. Parts of the program were most helpful. Some of the speakers were excellent. Not much pertained to the deaf-blind, and many theories on deaf education seemed so off-track.

In September, we prepared for Cara's move into the Deaf-Blind Unit at the W. R. MacDonald School. The school was 75 miles from our home in London. Cara would come home for weekends. Chuck and I were encouraged by the school staff to offer ideas and suggestions for activities. What did we see as short-term goals? What areas needed to be worked on? We felt very much a part of the program. During the first week, Cara and I visited "school" for a day. She met her teacher and three aids. We took her pretty pillow case to put on her bed. We took a favored doll, laundry bag, books, and some family pictures. Cara, from the beginning, always enjoyed school. She loved her teachers and friends, but this doesn't mean that the separation was easy. With such limited language, we could not tell her when we would come back, nor how long she would stay. Those first few months were a dreadful time for us. The car trips were heartbreakers. We couldn't face putting her on the school bus which transported the other children from our area.

Cara's first week at school was short. I drove her there on Wednesday morning, and left her with teacher, Sue. Cara's module of three had another girl and a boy Cara's age. This "module" shared a bedroom, classroom area, and activities directed by their teacher, assisted by three aids (residential counselors). The aids work on eight-hour shifts around the clock.

Of course, driving home from Brantford was the hard part, I had to stop several times to wipe away the tears. And, of course, I phoned the next morning. Jacquie told me that Cara cried a few minutes before falling asleep, but she was fine in the morning. I planned to pick her up at noon on Friday and would take her back Monday morning. I wasn't prepared for the way Cara greeted me on Friday. She totally pulled away. She wouldn't let me hug her. She didn't cry; she just ignored me. We got in the car to drive home, then the tears started. She cried until she slept. She was the same at home. She ignored everyone. We put the suitcase away and tried to do all the things she enjoyed doing at home. Cara withdrew into herself—pulling away from all of us. We were really frightened. What had happened to our girl? Was she so angry with us? On Saturday morning, the regular household activities went on with Cara watching but not involved. It was horrible. Then suddenly she started to cry and came to hug me. We were all so happy-sad that we were all crying and laughing. Even the dog was jumping around us. Cara was her old self again, until Monday morning when she saw the suitcase! I left her with Sue again. I checked with the school through the week to learn that Monday was a disaster with crying and tantrums, but the other days were very good. I picked her up on Friday and Sue asked if I would bring her back on Sunday so that she would be more settled when the Monday routine started. That's the way it went for the first few months. Our family drove Cara back on Sunday night after an early supper, and I picked her up on Friday. We were all tense and upset and aware of the empty place at home. Todd became afraid of the dark, even the dog started sleeping on Cara's bed.

When the road conditions became a problem in late November, I asked the school to send Cara home on the school bus. I'm sure she cried all the way home the first trip but was delighted to see me and soon was enjoying the bus rides.

In November, the Canadian National Institute for the Blind, in cooperation with the Deaf-Blind Unit at W. R. MacDonald School, held a national conference in Toronto. Chuck and I decided to go. The hard part was being away from Cara for the weekend. We gained so much from that conference. I believe it was the first time we had zeroed in on Cara's disability. We listened as other parents shared their experiences. A few doctors talked about rubella, the eye defects, neural disorders, heart, hearing, and other related problems. We met a few deaf-blind adults who attended with their interpreters.

We obtained some books and brochures on multisensory deprivation. John and Jacquie both made presentations. So much of what we heard made sense, and we heard so much that it took weeks to assimilate it all.

After Christmas we took Cara back to school. The residence was buzzing with activity. Cara was pleased to see her friends. Unlike many deaf-blind children, Cara and her best friend Laurel made a binding relationship. They interacted well. Cara was excited to see Laurel again. We met many other parents at that time. I remember one mother, who recognized our sadness at starting this new term, saying to us, "Those tears last until Easter. In a few years you will get so that you look forward to getting her off to school." I didn't believe it then, but there are times now when Sunday night is a blessing. And the best part is that I don't feel guilty about those feelings. It is hard work having Cara at home. We enjoy the activities we share. We love Cara's growth in independence and personality. We still shed a few tears as the bus leaves on Sunday night.

Summer holidays are an exciting part of everyone's year. Our summers have been made much more enjoyable through a program of "Summer Intervention." This is funded by government grants, and administered by the Canadian National Institute for the Blind with a great deal of input from our national association. Cara has an "intervener," a person chosen by us who understands this disability and is able to communicate with Cara. Together we plan activities: sports, community trips, crafts, and continue working on the school academic program. With her intervener Cara does everything from making Jello® to an all out camping adventure. Cara enjoys the independence that this allows and her development continues with added skills and new language.

This is Cara's story. Life seems to be a series of highs and lows. We try not to look to the future but deal one-day-at-a-time with Cara. Through the Canadian Deaf Blind and Rubella Association, we look to the future, working to improve conditions for deaf-blind persons across Canada. The task is gigantic, but, hopefully, each small step will lead us to the goal we seek. For deaf-blind persons, this means full-time intervention, so that each individual reaches his or her potential and becomes a part of the community.

Cara has finished six years in the deaf blind unit of the W. R. MacDonald School. Of course, the important gains are in the way of language. Cara is now able to express (in signs) her wants, needs, and ideas; and is able to understand our wants and ideas. (Very early she learned to shut her eyes if she didn't like what we were saying.) It is difficult to explain the kind of progress Cara is making. Sometimes we, ourselves, don't notice when Cara has moved on to more difficult tasks, or we become frustrated because she skips over some of the easy steps (continuing to ask for help), but at the same time is able to complete more difficult endeavors.

We are so thankful that we have the educational facility that challenges Cara. My philosophy has always been, "If Cara is happy she will learn, and if she is learning she will be happy." It's a matter of fulfilling oneself!

PSYCHOLOGICAL INTERPRETATION

Alan Balter

Cara's mother describes life after Cara's birth as a twelve-year journey consisting of a series of highs and lows. Indeed, a vivid sense of those mood swings is painfully apparent as one progresses through her narrative. Certainly, the fact that life is now relatively "easy" for this family and that Cara is at last well-adjusted and progressing at the MacDonald School are high points on the journey. However, the path to this plateau was so tortuous and so delayed by detours too often filled with callous and contradictory advice that it is surely not unreasonable to wonder how this family survived the trip at all.

One initial reaction to this family's story is outrage. To a physician whose quick comment has thus far caused eleven years of heartbreak, one wishes to ask, "Doctor, who is it that was deficient"? To a Ph.D. psychologist who would label a child with sensory handicaps "severely retarded" after one ill-planned and poorly executed testing session, one wishes to say, "Doctor, your testing was discriminatory." Of a system in which it was possible for one family to encounter twenty-eight different professionals, some of whose evaluations led to diametrically opposed opinions, one must wonder if its occasional successes result from intelligent progress through a systematized sequence or are simply due to a fortuitous combination of chance events.

The temptation to lash out in anger and point the finger of blame toward professionals whose technique and counsel seem ignorant and insensitive must be resisted, or at least tempered, for a number of reasons. First, it is easy, but unfair, to be critical of medical specialists and psychologists who are not present to offer a defense. Even in today's excessively litigious society, evidence would not be considered unless the defendants were available to rebut. Second, it is important to remember that this mother's recollections are subject to the same memory decay and subjectivity as any other's. In fact, a case could be made for the possibility that her anger, as fully justifiable as it might be, constitutes an added source of bias further clouding the truth. Third, and most important, even the most vehement expression of outrage would do nothing to undo the anguish this family has endured. What would likely have better effect would be a dispassionate analysis of the events and some reasoned suggestions for improving services to families in order to make their adjustments easier.

In large part, the reason for this family's difficulty was uncertainty. There was a five-year period of "not knowing" beginning in December, 1970. Motivated by a search for answers, the family engaged in a somewhat frantic, extended round of visits to more than two dozen professionals. During this search, which necessitated a job resignation, moving to another community, and leaving family and friends, the family felt frustration, anger, guilt, exhaustion, and what must have been considerable financial hardship. From their experience, a basic principle emerges: *In any system designed to deliver adequate services to families of handicapped children, uncertainty relative to present diagnosis and future educational placement must be held to an absolute minimum.* Given that this basic principle is valid, the question becomes one of implementation. What, specifically, needs to be provided to families to reduce their uncertainty and hasten their adjustment? The need for a professional to fill a central, integrating role is strikingly obvious. Whether the person is referred to as a case manager, facilitator, or professional advocate is not important; what is crucial is that the family have access to one person who can be relied upon to serve as the bulwark of their support system. This person needs to know of professional specialists in the community to whom the family could be appropriately referred and must be able to translate their findings and recommendations into language understandable to family members if need be. The case manager must know all of the special educational programs within the community as well as community agencies providing supportive services such as parent organizations, respite care facilities, vocational rehabilitation programs, and special recreation programs. Furthermore, the case manager must know the legislation applicable to the education and training of handicapped children and be able to advise parents relative to their specific rights. Finally, the case manager must be able to help the family plan for the future. Issues relative to financial planning and possible residential placement as the family ages must be considered.

The case manager might come from any one of a number of professions.

Whether trained as a social worker, pediatrician, special educator, or psychologist, it is imperative that the training include an internship during which the individual has direct and prolonged contact with handicapped children and their families. Preferably, during training, the professional will have lived with a family for a time and have experienced, on a first-hand basis, the profound effect that a handicapped child has upon the practicalities of everyday living for parents and siblings.

It is clear that case management involves awesome responsibilities as well as considerable training, knowledge, and experience. What is also clear is that families, whose dreams have been shattered and whose adjustment mechanisms are often fragile at best, will continue to flounder unless strong advocates are available to provide the cohesive and integrative force necessary.

JON

I am sitting in my son's third floor hospital room awaiting his return from major ear surgery. It is the middle of December, close to Christmas- ... and nearer still to Jon's eighteenth birthday. My God, how have we managed to survive eighteen years of deaf-blindness?

I have just spent the past several weeks gathering together medical and educational information and reviewing Jon's life as reported on paper by professionals for upcoming guardianship proceedings. To tell the truth, it has been a depressing endeavor as I read what these learned folks say about the flesh of my flesh and bone of my bone. I feel at low ebb.

The otolaryngologist enters our domain to relate that the operation went well and that the chaplain will soon escort me to the recovery room so that I may assist the staff in monitoring Jon's return from never-never-land. I look at my son lying there with oxygen mask hanging as an elephant-like appendage and his body shaking involuntarily from the anesthetic while skilled hands and eyes move from instrument to instrument. I ask myself, "What is reality? With whose reality am I forced to deal ... the written reports or my eighteen years of memories?" Traveling down memory lane is more nostalgia than I want to bear.

I have committed myself to write this chapter and I've always tried to meet my commitments, but to commit one's innermost thoughts to paper ... what a tremendous responsibility. To choose a portion of one's lifetime deemed interesting to others ... what a pompous supposition. To attempt to explain feelings and experiences to those who may not cross these bridges ... a fearful endeavor. Therefore, I shall walk very carefully, one step at a time, recalling my life with Jon ... much more carefully than we lived it, I admit.

It is my hope, while not my sole intention, that the reader may gain some small nugget from my comments which will make their pathway a little smoother.

I include the following essay written in 1978 and published by the

Dallas Times Herald as background information to relate a little about our family group. I feel it is a basis of comparison of my thinking then and now.

FOUR PLUS ONE EQUALS OUR FAMILY WITH JON

Jon-Jon walked across the room independently the other day. He is going through the decision-making "terrible two's." Jon-Jon is thirteen years old.

I wondered what the doctor was saying to me when at three weeks of age and in heart failure my third-born son was labeled "Rubella Syndrome." As the years have gone by Jon-Jon has earned the additional titles of "Deaf-Blind-Multihandicapped," "Severely and Profoundly Impaired," and "Developmentally Disabled." Our family has learned and lived with these descriptive phrases realistically.

Who would have thought that a simple childhood disease known as "German Measles" could inflict such havoc on the nerves of an unborn embryo? Jon survived the trauma of birth, fought back from heart failure and the rubella germ itself, was subjected to separate cataract removal operations on his eyes, plus corrective eye surgery, tolerated a trio of ear grommet implacements, and has been examined under anesthesia several times in his short thirteen years. Jon also wears short leg braces to correct an orthopedic problem and swallows medicine daily for sleep-awake disfunction.

During these thirteen years, our family has made necessary adjustments and priority selections that are different from those of our friends and neighbors, but maintaining a sort of family unity amidst the chaos of medical, educational, and social barriers. In our search for help, we have made four major household moves only to receive the usual "tsk-tsk" attitude from the field of medicine; a definite "sorry, no services available" from educators; the indifferent "You certainly do have a problem there, don'tcha" from the community.

We know the difference in our lifestyles without Jon, because on the advice of experts, we placed him in custodial care where he regressed, became skinny and unhappy. That tragic experience wasn't really the fault of the experts, for at that point in time, no one really knew what to do with a deaf-blind child. How do you invade his world of silent darkness to bring him out into your seemingly better world? No monies from private or governmental sources had thus far been made available to investigate our dilemma.

Although his natural father, who could not face the enormity, chose to retreat, Jon has a gentle, hardworking stepdad. His two older brothers have survived without notable psyche bruises. Both have won championship sport trophies. Both have exercised their creativity through art endeavors and the written word. Both graduated from their respective schools with honor grades. Both have found individual recognition performing in stage plays and musical presentations. Both are now furthering their education in their chosen fields. Both love their little handicapped brother; however, they have both been allowed the freedom to state that his handicap is bothersome, cumbersome, embarassing, and often discouraging. So it is.

Jon-Jon returned to his family four years ago and has made steady progress physically, mentally, and socially. Now there is professional expertise in the field of deaf-blindness. This year there are laws being implemented to educate the handicapped at their levels meeting their specific needs. These Individual Education Plans are executed by well-trained, dedicated, patient, empathetic teachers, aides, and therapists. Now there are supportive services available for parents, for families.

We still have a long way to go, as parents and siblings of handicapped individuals, working with our school systems and legislators, but having endured the struggle of the past thirteen years, as Jon-Jon's mother, I am confident I can manage the next thirteen, especially since I saw Jon walk across the room independently the other day.

Jon and I are both five years older now, time has not stood still. My hair is much grayer under my auburn rinse . . . Jon is much taller, uses daily deodorant, and is in need of a weekly shave. He is a young man in many ways while remaining severely and profoundly developmentally delayed. "Low Level" is a newer label he has acquired.

During the past five years, Jon and I both progressed. I have learned a great deal about special educators, service providers and how "to work within the system." Jon has learned that he can move around within his environment and that certain actions bring about certain responses.

My search for educational services for Jon began in 1965 soon after our return to the states from Lakenheath, England, where Jon was born an Air Force brat. In his file folder are answers to numerous inquiries I sent to such now famous institutes as The John Tracy Clinic, Perkins School for the Blind, Houston Speech and Hearing Center, Texas Education Agency, Callier Hearing and Speech Center, and etc. Most were sympathetic to my pleas but unable to assist us in a more tangible manner other than correspondence. They all recorded Jon as a statistic-...he is still a statistic.

Jon was two when we moved from San Antonio to Austin in hope that either the Texas School for the Blind or the Texas School for the Deaf, which are located there, would have some help available. Neither served the double sensory-deprived individual, and so it went. Deaf-blindness was not a popular cause...we are still a minority within a minority notwithstanding the "Rubella Bubble-Rubella Bulge" notoriety.

In June, 1968, the Austin CP Center evaluated Jon, giving me a spark of hope. The Director wrote many letters researching the availability of services and receiving similar negative responses. The CP Center did offer Jon some early childhood programming, but before this spark could be ignited, circumstances required our move to Dallas.

This was a traumatic sojourn for me and my sons. Our lifestyle altered abruptly as I became a single parent and head of the household. Re-entering the world of nine to five meant locating appropriate day care for Jon. Having already learned that service providers do not beat a path to one's door, I let my fingers do the walking, telephoning all over the metroplex until I found day care available at the CP Center on a sliding scale pay basis. Jon received no training, but they did keep him clean and dry. Inately I knew there should be someone out there to help me help him...I continued to hope and search in the midst of my working and mothering.

In the fall and spring of 1969, Jon was evaluated at Callier Center for Communication Disorders, which was then serving hearing and speech impaired persons but not the deaf-blind. It was their recommendations that led to our placing Jon in custodial care. Those years apart from Jon on a daily basis were probably the most difficult for me emotionally. Even though it gave us all a breather from the constant care of an S & P child, allowing me to spend more quality time with my other two sons, a part of me was forever missing.

I'd pop in at "Jon's home" bearing gifts, cling to him briefly, and then weep the twenty-five miles to my home, driving visually impaired. I doubt that anyone else knew my anguish or my aloneness regarding Jon. Why should they? I kept busy...busy with family, job, and church activities. My grief remained a private affair and Jon remained a statistic.

Because of the illness of Jon's natural father, causing his retirement from military service and a bureaucratic fluke, Jon's medical and custodial monetary assistance were terminated. Jon had just turned nine the previous December when I brought him home on a cold February morn and I was scared! Did I remember how to mother my own child after years of being just a visitor in his life? Those first forty-eight hours back in the nest were sleepless for me. I don't think I even blinked while watching his every move . . . checking his breathing, his temperature- . . . just as if he were a firstborn newborn. I decided, "What the hell, I can handle this"; I'd not forgotten how to nurture and love my own son whom I'd been yearning to mother. The void was filled. Jon was happy at home and I was happy with Jon. He gained healthy weight, grew taller, tanner, and more beautiful in just a few short months. We both glowed.

That May, I received a "home visit" from a Callier Center Team who informed me they had their deaf-blind program well established and were eager to include Jon. I was gun shy. I'd trusted too many experts in the past, saw my son regress, forget how to walk, and become emaciated. I knew I would never allow that to happen to him again, nor would I allow myself to watch it happen to him again. No, if they, the educators, couldn't best my most recent endeavors . . . uh-uh! They would have to now prove themselves to me. Jon would stay home.

God Bless the astute people that know when to push and when not to shove. The social worker member of the team was just such a person. She casually suggested that I attend a family-type conference sponsored by the regional deaf-blind center, to be held in Austin that July. She said I would have the opportunity to meet other parents of deaf-blind children and to compare notes. Following weeks of deliberation, I packed up seemingly half our household goods and Jon and the two of us traveled hesitantly back to Austin for the weekend retreat. She was right! I would never feel totally alone in my struggle for appropriate services for my son again. I would always have a compadre somewhere in this vast state who knew . . . KNEW what I was feeling, what I was facing . . . other parents . . . God Bless THEM! Other ding-a-ling deaf-blind kids . . . God Bless THEM!

Fall semester of 1974, Jon began his adventure into education at almost ten years of age. He had lost out on early intervention and early childhood services . . . but, he was to experience new concentrated input that would lead him toward new achievements for the rest of his life. Four years rocked by and Jon progressed, began reaching out beyond himself, became fairly mobile and self-ambulatory. I came to realize that Jon's sensory deprivation was and is an enormous disability but also, that he HAS abilities. He can, did, and does continue to learn.

I am in a continuing educational process, too. In my capacity as president of our statewide deaf-blind organization, I have had the opportunity to visit with many parents and to view many of the programs across the nation. I've learned a lot. I have gained the knowledge that most educators are stuck when their deaf-blind students reach their teens. "Suddenly" these kids are becoming young adults . . . their bodies prove it. The boys need occasional shaves, the girls need occasional sanitary napkins and both use daily underarm deodorant products. Their behaviors aren't considered "cute" anymore. Strangers, who once stared questioningly, now stare in dismay. Most classroom teachers are overwhelmed teaching 1970s strategy to 1980s students. They insist that their deaf-blind charges have reached a plateau, while I maintain it is the system which has plateaued. Splat!

Educators have been so busy with the daily chore of it all, they haven't pondered (as have most parents) the ever looming question, "What is going to happen to little Jackie once I'm gone?" Parents of older deaf-blind children have had to face the reality that they are not immortal! Their child will probably outlive them. Teachers feel that education lasts forever, while the reality is that in most states mandated education ceases at age twenty-one. Little Jackie will not remain in their classroom. The adult world awaits him and he isn't ready for it.

Teachers are still using simulated activities and objects when the reality is our kids need survival skills taught to them. Yes, train them to cope in the real world! When a deaf-blind child reaches the age of twelve, the community should begin to be his classroom. Age appropriate activities should be available to him no matter what his functioning level may be. Give our youngsters the opportunity to learn beyond the classroom setting or their growth will be stifled.

Educators need to open the door of their exclusive club and invite other service providers to participate in deaf-blind programming. Individual transitional plans need to be established so that our young adults will have a continuum of services and not end up rocking-chair bound, twiddling their thumbs. A deaf-blind child's educational program should be geared to what he will be doing after school age. Just as we all plan for the futures of our normal children from their birth, so we should begin planning for the futures of our disabled children.

Jon's present classroom is an extended living group home where he resides five days a week. (Jon and I still share our weekends.) From six o'clock Sunday evenings to six o'clock Friday, Jon is learning self-help skills and how to maneuver around in an independent living environment. He has four other deaf-blind housemates with whom he shares activities. This pilot project for lower functioning deaf-blind youths is located on one of the busiest streets in the heart of Dallas and the staff is beginning to access the community. For the most part, I am pleased with Jon's programming. I would like him exposed to a positive work activity and hope that will be forthcoming. I feel that the expectations of those in charge of carrying-out programming are still too low; however, I plan to keep encouraging the staff to allow Jon to develop and grow within this natural setting.

I feel that group homes or apartment living with supervision are the answer to our deaf-blind population's present and future needs and I hope this kind of innovative programming will continue. Oh sure, I get mad as hell the second time Jon spills his drink because he is not paying attention or is self-stimulating ... but I also am scared as hell when I think that he may not always have the opportunity to sit at his own dining room table and perhaps spill his drink.

What does the future hold for my son and his peers? My hope is beyond statistics.

PSYCHOLOGICAL INTERPRETATION

Georgia L. Granberry and Wayne Lasher

The question "Why" is a powerful tool for uncovering information in our everexpanding world. However, when that question becomes a crutch to lean on and a barrier to going forward with one's life, then the question should be changed to "What can we do now?". The mother of Jon has apparently long since moved on to the latter question and has found helpful if not entirely satisfactory answers as they apply to Jon's future.

Jon's mother has developed a focus centering on the present while laying the groundwork for the future. She has avoided the pitfall of devoting vast amounts of time and energy exploring the past. Questions of "Why is this happening to me?" or "What could I have done differently to prevent this from happening?" often invade the consciousness of parents. This can lead to frustration, guilt, and immobility. Meanwhile, the deaf-blind child is losing out on the care and attention that he or she so desperately needs.

Jon's mother has chosen to expend her energies in locating and utilizing what limited resources are available for the deaf-blind. She has experienced the frustration of little available knowledge on deaf-blindness, few facilities that can provide services, and a sometimes less than total commitment by governmental agencies and schools. However, her determination, in spite of all adversities, to find and utilize treatment and training that addresses Jon's abilities as well as his disabilities has led to the development of a philosophy that emphasizes the positive. This positive emphasis allows for Jon to go forward and learn whatever his potential may allow.

However, the road to maximum achievement possible for Jon is lined with impediments. The primary impediment is labeling. While it is essential to have universally accepted terms for lucid communication, it becomes a double-edged sword when the label distances the observer from the deaf-blind individual. It is easier to deal with a label than with an individual. Jon's mother has come into contact on many occasions with the world of labeling. These labels have sometimes provided professionals of the field with an excuse for saying, "Sorry, your child is deaf-blind; there is nothing that we can do for you or your child." It is apparent that Jon's mother has often felt the frustration of labels that close the door in her face. Being forced to communicate, if not accept, via labels has added another frustrating burden to an already very difficult situation. However, years of experience and learning have led her to the realization that working within the system provides for maximum benefits for all involved.

Another major impediment is the ambivalence toward professionals. Her feelings of frustration are not uncommon among families of deaf-blind. It would be of interest to know if she accepted the labels given to Jon by the professionals (i.e., doctors, educators, etc.) as the final answer to her inquiries or whether she requested that these professionals tell her what these labels meant in terms that had meaning to her. Often parents may feel intimidated by professionals and not push them for terms and information for their situation. This is not to say that parents should force professionals into a situation where they may feel attacked or obligated to provide explanations where cause and effect may be uncertain. Instead, parents should expect and work toward establishing a dialogue with professionals where a working relationship allows the exchange of valuable information.

Another major question to be considered by parents of the deaf-blind is "How much care and training, I as a parent, can I provide in the home and how much should I rely on outside resources?" The role of parents in the day-to-day training of the deaf-blind is often overlooked. Every activity or situation that the deaf-blind child encounters holds potential as a learning activity. Parent education to train parents as teachers of their deaf-blind children need not be overly complicated or confusing. Consistency and repetition are the keys to learning and can be easily transmitted to motivated parents.

It is a sad fact that many parents shortchange themselves and their handicapped child by using some of the same catch phrases as professionals: "He's deaf-blind, I don't know what to do." Parents, if they have other children, should be asked this question, "What did you do to teach your other children?" All children can learn and many learning activities can be adapted to the deaf-blind. It would be of interest to know how much home training was in Jon's daily routine and how much was reserved for outside the home. The parents as trainers are a very valuable resource that is too often overlooked. Overreliance on professionals for training can have the effect of minimizing a handicapped child's development.

The last major question for the parents of a deaf-blind individual to ask and/or answer is "What is going to happen to little Jackie once I'm gone?". Jon's mother has every right to be concerned over this question. Education should not be a goal in itself and education should not end just because the child reaches 21 years of age. Educators have begun to realize that education/training for individuals over 21 years of age can be beneficial and effective. Adult education/training in the areas of self-help skills, daily living skills, social/recreation/leisure skills, and survival language skills has the potential for teaching adult deaf-blind further refinement of existing skills and abilities. These basic skills provide a framework in learning that has potential for prevocational/ vocational skills acquisition and for leading to appropriate vocational placement. Acquiring vocational skills can provide a way to structure for the deaf-blind at least part of their day, to attain the least restrictive living environment, and hopefully to assist in providing financial support for their care. Even the severely and profoundly handicapped have proven to be capable of learning tasks that have vocational potential. Vocational training, as well as self-help training, should be designed to utilize Jon's strengths and should be reviewed constantly in an ongoing process. Short-term as well as long-term goals should be considered as a collaborative effort of both parents and professionals.

The emotional up and down of dealing with a deaf-blind individual and his unique needs has certainly molded or at least altered the personality of Jon's mother. Having two other children provides her with joy and pride in their achievements. However, her pleasure with Jon's accomplishments is no less than the pleasure she receives from her other children's achievements. The goals for Jon may be much smaller, but the struggle to obtain those goals brings with it a heightened sense of enjoyment when Jon accomplishes his goals. Her personal philosophy may be best described as one of acceptance. This acceptance does not allow for blame or denial. Instead, it allows for accepting life just as it is and continually striving to assist her child's development to his maximum potential.

DEAN

Throughout Dean's life we have had to face many frustrating years without help, especially education, which we feel would have provided a breakthrough in helping him to communicate, and to be accepted into this so-called normal world.

I am certain that if Dean had been born with just one specific handicap, then he would have been accepted into a school that catered to that handicap. Because he was unfortunate enough to be born multiply-handicapped, then from the very start he was doomed to be classed as severely subnormal, and that label has lived with him on all his records right up until this very day.

At the age of 4½ years, Dean went for a month's assessment at Sunshine Home for the Blind, which decided his handicaps were too severe for him to remain there. So back he came to our own borough to attend a training center, which in the early 1960s was run by Social Services. None of the staff were trained, and the ages of the many different handicaps who attended there ranged from four to forty or even older.

The children in those years did not have to be educated, so Dean spent many wasted years with about 18 different handicapped children, just lying on the floor playing with his hands which he was content to do, just living in his twilight world. Even though I knew Dean was not getting the help that he needed, I had to accept this, having two children younger and one a bit older. When I asked about education, I was told that I had to be thankful that Dean was looked after during the day.

Because I was certain his hearing was not perfect, we were sent, when he was five years old, to the Nuffield Speech and Hearing Center, which I'm afraid I did not find very helpful. I did ask if they would write to my borough to ask for a home teacher of the deaf to attend the training center and work with Dean.

After many months without help, a teacher did arrive, but only came once a month. After complaining that this just was not enough time, she started attending on a fortnightly basis, but I had no help with Dean at home during the holidays. The teacher, unfortunately, had never been trained to teach a multiple handicapped child, so I am afraid progress was very slow.

When Dean was seven, I wrote to the Ministry of Education and Science in London to ask if he could possibly go to a school that catered to his handicaps, and after many frustrating months the authorities decided to send him for a six-month assessment to the Helen Terry Home for the blind and subnormal in Reigate.

Even though his progress was very slow, we thought that he was beginning to become a little more independent, but once again our hopes were dashed when at the end of the six-month period they told us they could not keep him because they had so many other handicapped children to assess. So once more, back he came to the training center, where he stayed without much help until at the age of 10 years, education became compulsory for all mentally handicapped children.

The coming of education for these children was a great step forward. They built a nice new school which was now called "Shestone Special School", and staffed it with well-trained teachers. I am afraid, however, it came too late for the likes of Dean and others who could not communicate.

By the time Dean was 15 years, he seemed to be really picking up, but sadly, at 16 he had to leave, so once again the good work that he had gained in the last year was all undone. I asked if Dean could stay on because the Adult Training Center was full, and all they would offer me was a mental hospital not far from my home, but the answer was no, because they must make way for the younger ones coming along. By now they were taking children in at 2½ years. Of course, I felt very bitter about this because Dean was the only one to leave that Easter, and they could have let him stay on to the Summer, when a hostel would be opening.

I feel certain I was victimized because I would not accept the mental hospital placement. They told me there was no help for Dean in any way. For three whole months I had Dean home every day and he became so frustrated that he smashed his head through my glass cabinet and through my back door. He smashed his head everywhere, bit all his clothes to pieces, and he bit and scratched me so that my arms were covered with bruises. I feel certain that God at this time gave me the strength to go on, and not give in to the authorities who wanted to send Dean to the mental hospital. Without His help I myself would have become a mentally disturbed person.

By chance, one day I happened to meet a counselor who had a mentally handicapped son of his own, and he decided that help must be given to me. He managed to get Dean into a hostel that was now open three days a week from 10:00 A.M. to 2:30 P.M. It's disgusting how authorities treat you, for once again Dean went back to just being looked after, they said I must be thankful for small mercies for there was nowhere else for him to go.

He stayed at the hostel on a three-day basis for about two years, and then our Rubella Society opened their first residential home for adults. We were "over the moon" when he was accepted at "Market Deeping." We thought he would be going on a six-month assessment, but once again due to Dean's terrible tantrums, he only lasted five weeks, so once more he came back to the hostel.

One day a small advertising paper was put through my door, and I read about an illness called Gilles de la Tourette syndrome, of which the symptoms are face twitches, head jerking, arm jerking, feet stamping, over breathing, head banging, the making of all kinds of noises and also repetitive movements, which in Dean's case meant that all the doors must be shut right up, all the jars on the shelf had to be put in a straight line, and there had to be not one button undone on my husband's shirts. I knew that Dean had all these symptoms, but was told over and over again it was because he was severely subnormal and "you must put up with what he does." I had never seen another Rubella person react like Dean did, so I decided to write to the chairman of this association, who came to visit us and felt Dean could be helped by the medication that is given to these sufferers. It was a blessing in disguise, because after a few months of taking Serenace, Dean became more tolerable to live with. Why, then, did we have to wait until he was 18 years old before there was help for him?

Just over a year ago Dean started at a new adult training center, The Smerdon Center, which was named after the counselor who had helped me in the beginning.

Dean now goes daily, but is only in the special care class, which I am certain is because of the lack of training over the years. We still feel that if Dean had had the right training for his multiple handicaps, he would still be trainable; he would never have been brilliant, but this we did not want, only for him to be more independent.

Looking back, my husband and I often wonder how we have survived what he calls "The Rubella Years." Our biggest worry is what will the next twenty years bring? We both hope that something will come out of the blue after all for Dean, and that his precious life on Earth is not wasted. He may not have contributed much, but not through any fault of his, but through the lack of understanding of people in authority.

I pray that Dean goes before we do, because I could not bear the thought of him going into a mental hospital, for he's always been brought up in our home environment and he has given us a lot of love and understanding and made better people of us all.

PSYCHOLOGICAL INTERPRETATION

Kevin D. Magin

Dean's story and that of his parents represent an all too familiar scenario in the annals of the education of severely handicapped individuals. Parents the world over have looked at the services of today and felt the frustration expressed by Dean's mother. To be faced with the reality of the advent of educational services too late to provide maximum benefit to one's child serves to only increase the frustration of years of looking, prodding, probing, and demanding that these services be available, can be provided, and must be provided to the Dean's of the world.

However, looking to the past will not benefit Dean or others to follow unless we look to the historical with a perspective to the future. Given the current level of services at any time, we can and must exercise a commitment to provide that which is viable in the most effective manner. By looking at Dean's mother's account, we can benefit by examining our current service delivery systems in light of many of her comments.

The undertone of frustration of Dean's mother can be seen in two poignant statements in her story. "It's disgusting how authorities treat you . . . " and " . . . through the lack of understanding of people in authority."

It is the responsibility of the service provider agencies and organizations and especially those in mandated authority to be aware that the parents of severely handicapped children often are groping for answers and help while struggling to maintain the best environment they can give without benefit of training and experience. Dean's mother expressed this position by telling us, "Even though I knew Dean was not getting the help that he needed, I had to accept this, having two children younger and one a bit older. When I asked about education I was told that I had to be thankful that Dean was looked after during the day."

We cannot, even in today's more sophisticated educational climate, provide services that do not exist; however, we can be expected to be cognizant of the situations these parents are facing and exhibit behaviors that express our concern and care for the child and family. We can be expected to be professionally responsible and assist the parents to the extent possible rather than contribute yet another source of frustration.

The behaviors and attitudes we present to parents can of themselves relieve much of the anxiety and frustration. The thought that someone else cares, someone else will help, someone else knows what we are going through can ease the immense task facing these parents.

Aside from the attitudes we portray, we need to insure that our service delivery system includes the maximum services, qualified and trained personnel, and facilities commensurate with the child's needs. Even more tragic than not having services is having services available and not making those needing these services aware of their existence. Severely handicapped children do not come equipped with a list of service organizations or agencies. Each professional who comes in contact with the parents of a severely handicapped child is obliged to provide his or her service to benefit the child and family to the maximum extent available. Additionally, he/she must assist in directing the parents to other appropriate service providers and in alerting those service providers of the needs of the child and family. Dean's story is one of the parents constantly searching for services. There is nothing wrong with services going in search of children and families.

Perhaps the last issue we can learn from Dean's story is that we must inform the parents not only of services available now but the continuum of services available upon reaching certain age or developmental levels. Parents need to plan for tomorrow as well as live for today. Each program Dean entered seemed to magically appear and this may be true given the time frame of Dean's development. In today's hopefully more developed days, we should be in a better position to explain a continuum as well as alternative services available. Hopefully, this will allow us to decrease the anxiety expressed at the close of Dean's story. Spending a lifetime to develop services for one's child only to feel that it would be better for him/her to pass away before you because of lack of a continuum of services may be the ultimate in frustration.

We can and we must listen to the Dean's mother's of the world and provide not only better services but the hope that these services will ally the fears of the passage of time and allow parents to enjoy their years with their children, secure in the knowledge that these special children will continue to have others to assist them as they grow and progress.

DONALD

Mother's Story

We are parents who have fought the "system" for 25 years. We think we have helped change some things for handicapped children, but we have yet to see much change in society's attitude toward those who are "different."

Our story has no ending—yet. I am very envious of parents whose children have overcome serious handicaps and are comfortable with their condition.

Our adult, legally blind-deaf, 28-year-old son was educated primarily in public schools (in keeping with the principle of normalization, although we started 15 years before P.L. 94-142 was enacted). People who know Don have said it is remarkable that he has come so far with limited vision and a hearing impairment that has progressed to deafness. But now that he is ready to go out into the world of employment, there seems to be no place for him. (All handicapped persons need to feel that they are worthwhile and that they can make a contribution to society.)

Don has had much vocational rehabilitation training since leaving college—although no effort was made by VR to "counsel" him during his college career as to what field might be best for him; no aptitude tests were given, no job search was undertaken or internship or on-the-job training in his academic major (journalism) during all of his college years. I feel that this is an area that should be an integral feature in preparation for full-time employment.

During summer vacations, Don worked as a volunteer in several jobs, e.g., a mental hospital where he talked with women waiting to get into the alcohol rehabilitation program. They read poetry to each other, played pool, and just talked. He worked in a cerebral palsy center where he played with the kids, went on field trips, etc. He was also employed 10 weeks in the deaf-blind unit of a state institution for the retarded.

Don does not have a very good idea of what is expected of him in a work situation. He feels that he is ready to work, but many employers do not have the patience to train a multihandicapped person.

Don has used braille since the first grade in school. He had a devoted braille teacher who realized he had peripheral vision and taught him to read large print as well as braille. He could not hear well enough to participate in the classroom discussions, but he said it was worth going to school just to see the pretty girls. Most of his teachers, and later his counselors at public school, did not understand his psychological needs. They didn't realize that he needed a kind word or a little pat on the back, not just screaming in his face. An English class was reading stories by Poe and the teacher told Don they were going to read "Tell Tale Heart." He asked her several times and she just kept repeating "Tell Tale Heart" louder and louder in his face. When he told this incident to me, he said that he understood the words but he just didn't know what they meant.

Since he was three or four years old, Don has not been able to understand conversation among several people. When you know people are talking and all you hear is a jumble of sounds, you become frustrated. Because of the problem of "audio-processing," many words would not be heard by Don in their correct form. For example, when he was about six years old he was singing "dig that manger scene" one Christmas and we finally realized that's what he heard in "and Heaven and Angels sing." We had his hearing tested three different times by an ENT doctor and the test results always showed he could hear. At that time he *could* hear one word spoken into earphones, but there didn't seem to be any way of testing what he understood when a whole sentence was spoken to him.

During this time, his teachers insisted he could "hear when he wants to."

Children's Hospital in Washington, D.C. tested his hearing many times when he was 10 years old and finally "discovered" that he had a problem. Even then, each test had a different result and no recommendations for aid were offered.

We asked Children's Hospital to send a report of Don's hearing test to the junior high school so the teachers would have "proof" of his hearing loss.

Although Don couldn't use his hearing in the classroom, he was able to hear enough at home on a one-to-one basis to develop good language and speech. With his father's help, he expanded his vocabulary as he grew up. I learned braille while Don was in kindergarten, as we knew his optic nerve was atrophied because of encephalitis at age nine months. Don's father taught him geography by outlining large maps with felt tipped pens and I identified the large cities and important areas of each country with braille signs pasted on the map. Don's vocabulary grew as he read many nonfiction books in braille and then would discuss the subjects with his father. He still gives his dad "pop" quizzes like, "What is the name of the official residence of the President of South Korea?" (The Blue House)

Don is very frustrated with his life and has some very strong emotions about the way he feels he is treated, even by people who work with the handicapped.

He was a very caring and loving youngster. When someone offered him candy or a balloon, he always asked for one for his older brother. Brother Bob is 4½ years older than Don and as a young child was very jealous of the attention that Don required. It has taken many years for Bob to understand Don's needs, but he can now sincerely say to Don, "I love you." Bob has become proficient in the manual alphabet in order to communicate with Don.

Don was able to keep stride with the neighborhood children until he was about 10 years old. Then he would come in crying and say they wouldn't let him play because he was blind. One way that Don could join in activities with his peers was at the swimming pool. His father had a lifeguard teach him the basic swim strokes by moving his arms and legs in the water. Don then swam on the Class A team in our area for several years and swam medley (four different strokes). He was very faithful in attending practice daily every summer and the swim meets on Saturday, but he was still sometimes an "outsider." The other kids couldn't talk to him, but would assist him on occasion. He missed most of the jokes and the camaraderie that go with group activity.

One of the questions asked most frequently by professionals is "how did you feel when you learned your son was partially sighted and would need to use braille?" I have never been able to answer that question. I don't know if I just don't remember, or I don't want to remember. I just know that I began looking around for a braille class and prepared myself to help him when he needed me.

I might mention here that our first child was born about 8 years before Bob. She seemed like a very normal baby, but at six months of age a congenital tumor was discovered on her sacroiliac which was to become a medical problem the rest of her short five-year life. Sometimes, if I let myself think about it, I have to wonder why "bad things happen to good people."

Concurrent with Don's enrollment in college, he and I began sign language classes. Interpreters attended class with Don all through his college years and he had tutors and notetakers to augment the lectures. I transcribed all of his notes into braille during this time. None of Don's tutors and very few of his friends knew sign language, but they used a Telatouch machine which is a device to communicate with the deaf-blind. Don's father communicates with him using only the manual alphabet, as he thinks it is more precise than signing.

Some of you who read this and know Don will remember him as being intelligent, able, and very eager to share his abilities with others. But with the passage of time, Don feels more and more isolated.

I hope the time will come when the professionals who work with the handicapped will realize that each person has to be treated in a very special way and cannot be made to fit the textbook mold. They each have different social and psychological needs that must be dealt with. The professionals who have worked with Don since he graduated from college have not been warm and empathetic, but have demanded more of him than was reasonable. This is not to say that there are not many fine professionals out there who try very hard within the confines of their job. I feel that Don is capable of doing more than he has done so far, but he is so emotionally exhausted that his social skills are maladroit. Don says he keeps trying, but nothing seems to work. He reacts very well when someone shows that they care about him, but he does less well if he perceives people as uncaring. Maybe we led him to expect more than it was possible to attain. I still think there is a caring, capable human being inside Don. I only pray that he gets the opportunity soon to prove this. To paraphrase a TV commercial, "A mind is a terrible thing to waste."

At this writing (winter 1982) Don is working temporarily at the National Library Service for the Blind and Physically Handicapped, Library of Congress. The personnel there have been very encouraging and very patient and understanding of his frustrations.

We still believe in "normalization" and will continue to work for the rights of the handicapped and to lessen societal barriers.

Father's Story

The time was Spring, 1955. Our son, Don, was nine months old. He and his mother were visiting relatives in Oklahoma City. I joined them after a business trip and I noticed that there was a slight "quiver" (nystagnus) in Don's eyes and he had a mild rash. He was hospitalized, his condition worsened for a couple of days, then his symptoms subsided, and in a few days he was back home in Washington, D.C.

This was my first of many "significant" exposures to medical doctors with Don. Although Don was a private patient, with private doctors, they chose to run no tests (e.g., spinal tap) that might have provided definitive data as to the cause and nature of his illness. When I suggested that it might be appropriate to undertake such procedures—after they had had more than enough time to do so—I was given the treatment usually afforded lay people who have the temerity to question the infallability of medical doctors. The doctor and I had a heated and an essentially fruitless exchange. Precious time was lost, the damage had been done and was irreversible. Some years later the illness was "diagnosed" as encephalitis.

During the first three or four years of Don's life, we had a great many tests run (e.g., neurological, opthamological, etc.) in an attempt to establish with a fair degree of certainty the nature and extent of his impairments and strengths.

After collecting data, we then had to decide where we thought he should go to school, where he should live, what support systems he would need, how well the "establishment" would accomodate his needs, and how it would attempt to reject him.

We had no illusions about the lack of empathy or understanding that he would encounter from the power structure. We knew that it was, and is, configured to accomodate "normal" people and that it does not look kindly on those who are different. We made this assumption going in. We were proved correct. However, we felt that the alternative— institutionalization—was worse. Yes, a state school for the deaf or the blind—however you cut it—is an institution. We rejected the conventional wisdom that said that your child had to attend such a school. We insisted that he attend his local school with peers from his own neighborhood.

The year was 1960 and it was time for Don to begin his formal education. The first two years he attended his local grade school. An itinerant teacher taught him the basics of braille and print. Parenthetically, his mother learned braille before he started to school and later learned sign language. She did so not only to assist him with his special needs, but also to deny the public school system the opportunity to cashier him because he didn't have braille books. In the third, fourth, and fifth grades, he attended a public school some distance from home. This placement enabled him to sharpen his braille skills. He was driven to and from school each day. The two exceptions to public school education were two months in a state school for the blind (where we were repeatedly assured he would get individual attention because of his hearing loss). The other exception was a year in a private prep school where he *did* receive one-to-one instruction (Algebra, Spanish, etc.) which enabled him to make a successful transition from junior high school to senior high.

One has to be prepared to deal with the endless means that society, especially the public schools, uses in an attempt to deny your child his rights under the Constitution and as a human being. First, establish the facts, without stint or favor, as they pertain to your child. Otherwise, you cannot be an effective advocate. Know what cards you hold and those that your adversary holds. Be prepared to counter his ploys with a stronger suit, whether you have to wait a day or ten years. In fact, it may be advantageous, in the short run, to let him think he is winning. Many "lost" battles can be tactical retreats for the purpose of disarming your adversary.

The following illustrates some specific "battles":

Item: The state school for the blind was a predictable disaster. Don was assaulted by older boys and was held under a shower by a house parent as punishment for something that he had not done. After the incident, I checked the facts and the law very carefully. After establishing the facts, I withdrew Don from the state institution and he was returned to his neighborhood school.

Item: When Don was in the 7th grade, kids would kick him and run away. He wanted me to go over and "take care of them" (i.e., physically). I told him I couldn't do that, but that I could equip him to handle the problem. A wrestling instructor came to our home and gave him lessons in karate and wrestling for about three months. Don was also working out with weights. His instructor informed me when he felt Don could take care of himself. I told Don that the next time he was kicked to quickly grab the kid and "beat the hell out of him." He was kicked again and he whipped not only one, but two kids. That took care of the problem.

Item: Corporal punishment was used against Don by a junior high school principal. My wife and I made an appointment to visit him (It is important that most things are made a matter of record). The stated purpose of the visit was simply to discuss our son's progress. After doing so, we asked the principal if there was anything else that he would like to discuss. The answer was no. I then mentioned the matter of corporal punishment and asked if he had, in fact, not broken the law. He ordered us out of his office, but I told him I would rather pursue the matter at his level, unless he wished me to speak with the superintendent of education for the county. He then became very cooperative. I told him that I was only interested in him serving the interests of my child and that I would like him to call me once a week and give me a progress report. The fact here is that he had compromised himself by breaking the law.

Item: When Don was to enter senior high school, we were asked to wait until the school had held a "building conference" about his placement. I learned from private and reliable sources that an assistant superintendent of education was going to recommend that Don be returned to the state school for the blind. Immediately upon learning of this, I called Don's medical doctor (counselor) and informed him of what I had learned. I asked him if he felt that the state school would be a proper placement for Don and he said "no." I then asked if he would call the school principal and tell him so. This he did. The principal informed me that Don could begin attending school the next day. At my request, the board of education assigned a special teacher to work with Don 10 hours a week on a one-to-one basis at the school. The Doctor was brought into the picture because there are times when the most effective way of dealing with a specialist (principal) in the power structure is with a higher order specialist. What school principal wants to run the risk of a lawsuit by ignoring the advice of a medical specialist.

Item: By the time that Don was ready to enter the 11th grade, we had moved to Oklahoma. Before doing so, we received assurances in writing and in person, that he would be accepted by the high school. His mother spoke with a number of Oklahoma school principals in person and I corresponded with the state department of education. A school did accept Don and he did well. He was on the principal's honor roll.

At a meeting with the state department of education and others, the department representative recommended that Don take an extra year to finish high school because it would be too difficult to complete in a two-year period with his disabilities. I asked him if he knew that Don was taking a full course load and that he was on the principal's honor roll. He said that he didn't and since that was the case, he would withdraw his recommendation.

Item: Don was given an SAT test (Scholastic Aptitude Test—required for college entrance). He took the test orally and his score was low. I called the local SAT representative and asked him how many deaf-blind people had taken the test. He said he had no data on that, but that nothing could be done about it because the information was "already" in the computer. He also informed me that I wasn't talking to just any guy on the street. He said, "I have a Ph.D." I then called the main office in another state and talked with a woman who was very understanding and wrote a letter to the university to say that the test had no validity in Don's case. A carbon copy was sent to the "Ph.D."

Item: A more pleasant note. Don entered the University of Oklahoma in 1973 and graduated in 1980. At that level, it took longer to complete a baccalaureate since all of his books had to be brailled, his notes brailled (by his mother), and we had to find interpreters and notetakers for each class and tutors for some. He was graduated with a 3.5 grade average and a 3.7 in his major.

The difference in the attitude of teachers and administrators toward a deaf-blind student below the college level and the attitude of those at the college level is as different as highnoon and midnight. There was not a teacher or an administrator at the University level who didn't welcome Don enthusiastically. Many would say, "It would be an interesting challenge to have Don in class." They were accessible and they went out of their way time and again to accomodate his special needs. That is not to say that all those below the college level wore black hats. There were many during those years who were dedicated, supportive, and a credit to their professions. Unfortunately, they were the exception, not the rule.

Item: Post College

This period is perhaps the most heartrending, disappointing, and most enlightening to me regarding Don's life. He has moved from subsystems or entities, (e.g., high school and college) that are fairly tractable and easy to control, to society at large, which, of course, is infinitely complex and hydra-headed.

Item: The statement of a state superintendent for the school for the deaf. "Don, you have an excellent resume and transcript and I would hire you in a minute, but you are deaf-blind."

Item: Letter written to Don by a principal at a school for the deaf-blind in a southeastern state when Don was seeking employment. "It has been my experience that the deaf-blind do not find gainful employment."

What then must we do? We must fight to keep our hardwon opportunities. Recognize that, at the moment, the federal laws that support the handicapped are in jeopardy. A few of the present dangers are the elimination of block grants, the elimination of specific rights by re-writing or eliminating federal regulations (i.e., IEP's), reductions in funds, etc.

Again, let me say, we must access the system. We must make it work for us. We must run it rather than have it run us. We cannot do this without knowing how it works. Therefore, work with, but never become a captive of, those who help to determine who gets what and when. We must learn who our friends are, real and potential. Become acquainted with advocacy groups at the local, state, and national level. Join them. Stand close enough to learn the circuitous, arcane, and self-serving ways in which the system "works." Become privy to its secrets but never permit yourself to be compromised by becoming an official paid member of the system. Do not be intimidated by threats made against you or become cynical by the manipulation, scapegoating, and denial that exists. Realize that those things that unite us are greater than those that divide us. Know those who affect your interest, from courthouse to Congress. If they are on your side, work for them. If they are neutral, try to explain the correctness of your cause. After all, a great many people who affect your interests, know very little about "special" education. However, many are willing to learn. If you encounter those who are irrevocably opposed to your interests, neutralize them. Work openly or clandestinely to defeat them. Is this easy? No. Can it be done? Yes.

Power is a heady potion. It comes in many forms — knowledge, access, timing, commitment, endurance, money, and risk-taking.

Do not be beguiled into believing that those who hold power will surrender it peacefully and gracefully because it is the right and decent thing to do.

Ironically, billions have been spent on and by those who are supposed to be advocates for our children. However, if you do not acquire power, in your own right, you will perforce have to play by the rules of those gatekeepers in our society who determine the rights of passage.

Get involved. Become active. Participate in the development of the rules. Never lose sight of the ultimate objective — the winning of the war.

Item: I worked for well over a year to change the definition of Develop-mental Disabilities (P.L. 94-103) to include the deaf-blind. As 94-103 was written, it was limited to some four specific disabilities—the largest of which, by number, were the retarded.

I wrote a letter to the president of the state council to ask if deaf-blind could be included. He wrote me and said no. I then wrote a letter to the regional representative and asked the same question. I was told no. My third letter was written to an officer in HEW, who was responsible for developmental disabilities and again I was told no. I was doing two things. I was getting letters (documentation) that the developmentally disabled wanted no part of us. I was also exhausting every administrative remedy, which you sometimes need to do to make a legal case. I then wrote to the U.S. senator in charge of legislation for the handicapped and sent copies of the letters that I had received. He passed the problem to HEW for action who in turn passed it to a consulting firm which is concerned with such. They called me in Oklahoma and asked if I would prefer to add deaf-blind or to change the definition to fit all developmentally disabled. I indicated a preference for the latter. That way no developmentally disabled person would be excluded. The law was changed and is now Public Law 95-602.

A fact which needs to be kept in mind is how much time a given problem may take. Some are thirty second-type problems and some are thirty months. If you don't make some realistic assessment as to how long it may take to resolve a problem, you will soon be overwhelmed with frustration, anger, and anxiety.

If my account or story strikes you as cynical or "downbeat," so be it. As far as I am concerned, it is simply realistic.

My wife and I have been in the "trenches" for twenty-five years. We have held office in organizations for the deaf-blind at the local, state, regional, and national levels.

I have actively worked (e.g., testified) for the enactment of a great deal of legislation (e.g., P.L. 95 142, The Education for All Handicapped Children Act) that hopefully has helped the deaf-blind.

I teach political science at the college level, have worked on Capitol Hill and am a U.S. Foreign Service Officer (retired) from the Department of State.

I think I have a passing acquaintance with the way that the system works.

Is there anything that we can do while we await the arrival of the millennium? Of course there is.

Let us assault the loneliness and isolation that engulfs our children.

Let us send them summer, show them sunshine. Let us give them joy and love and let them taste each day, a bit of life's sweetness.

They must never become the victims of a dream deferred, a place too far, or a time too late.

PSYCHOLOGICAL INTERPRETATION

Pearl E. Tait

Don's parents are early pioneers in the integration of handicapped individuals into the mainstream of American society. They began their work, before Public Law 94-142 was available to offer them support, when they made the decision to have Don attend his local school with peers from his own neighborhood. This decision, their efforts to maintain Don successfully in an academic environment, and their advocacy efforts have had an impact on all those who follow them.

Unfortunately, just as the early pioneers crossed the Mississippi only to face the Rocky Mountains, Robert and Charlene realize that even though they have helped Don through the hurdle of academia, Don is faced with new challenges. Academic success can be attained by passing tests, completing a certain number of courses, etc., and Don's parents were instrumental in the successful accomplishment of these goals. However, the steps to successful employment and social well-being are not so clearly defined. They are dependent upon such things as "getting along with others" and "presenting a good image." Also, Don's parents are less able to help him overcome obstacles. Don is at that stage in life when, like most young adults, he must strive to distance himself from his parents. However, successful independence requires employment, and a growing circle of friends and acquaintances. While many young adults face this stage with some anxiety, the task for someone with a vision and hearing loss is much more difficult.

The frustration felt by the family is evident. Even though Don has achieved the goal they once envisioned would open the door to society, they find that it has simply brought them to another door—the transition from school to work. Realistically, the problems brought about by the dual loss of vision and hearing do not go away, they simply change as the individual goes through life's stages. Each stage brings with it different problems.

49

Parents and concerned professionals can work together to help make the transitions easier. The U.S. Department of Education recognizes the problem and supports grants for innovative model programs to help in the transition. Parent groups are organizing to provide support for their children as they move out of the school system. As the first wave of Public Law 94-142 students reaches the threshold, it becomes evident that what was seen as a culmination is only a beginning.

The father has been very active in utilizing legal issues and fighting for legislation. There is, I believe, a rather naive notion in our society that legislation can solve problems. As is evident from many forms of discrimination, this is not so. Discrimination, whether by race, sex, or disability, is dependent on the attitudes of society. Legislation, while it indicates a move toward a change in attitudes, does not automatically change attitudes toward any group. However, it does create opportunities for attitudes to change. But attitudes change slowly. Attitudes toward disabled individuals will only change gradually as more people have positive contacts with disabled individuals who have strong self-images. Also, as disabled individuals are presented with more successful models, they will in turn be more apt to see themselves in a positive light. In this way, television has the potential to accomplish as much as, if not more, legislation in changing attitudes. Talk shows discussing the problem of being "different" in our society, series that include successful lawyers and comedians who are disabled, individuals who achieve in sports, all present more positive images of disabled individuals. They are no longer depicted as helpless and weak beings at the mercy of those around them, but as strong people, who, given half a chance, will prove themselves.

Individuals function daily within a framework predetermined by the attitudes they hold. They are also influenced by attitudes held by others toward them. Robert's story very clearly portrays a belligerent, adversarial position of parent vs. school system, certainly with justification. However, there is the old saying: "When you ask for a fight, you get it." Would the story have changed to a degree if the parents had not entered negotiations with the school system with a preconceived negative assumption? Institutions are made up of people, and people respond to anger with anger. It has been stated that the way in which parents first learn of their child's condition appears to contribute greatly to the way in which parents handle the situation. Usually the physicians are the first to break the news to the parents. Horror stories abound. In this case, you can identify with the anger and frustration of the parents as they see their child damaged by an illness, the effects of which might have been lessened *if they had been listened to.* No wonder the parents do not passively accept what others have to say about Don's welfare. They had no reason to trust others. The seeds of anger and distrust had been planted very early.

Professionals, as individuals, also hold the attitudes of the society in which they live regardless of their membership in the school system. Teachers, administrators, and psychologists, even though they are in the business of serving children, have their attitudes toward the disabled individuals formed largely by the society in which they live. If their society holds the view that disabled children are not "normal" or "cannot learn," professionals will also be governed by these attitudes. Their attitudes do not change simply by "becoming" a teacher, a psychologist, or an administrator. Professionals are, after all, cut from the same cloth as the rest of society.

At the time when Don was attending school, classroom teachers and psychologists were not required to have knowledge about disabled children. Five years after the passage of PL 94-142, only 15 states required some exposure to the characteristics and needs of exceptional children and youth.[1] Even today only 33 of the 50 states require at least a survey course in the education of exceptional children for teacher certification.[2] Psychologists who have a long history of separating the "normal" and "abnormal," have only since February of 1985 established, by the governing body of the American Psychological Association, a continuing Committee on Psychology and Handicaps. This committee is charged with representing the interest and concerns of persons with disabilities within APA and within the broad field of psychology. During Don's education, few people in the system had any knowledge or experience with disabled children. This was clearly compounded by the fact that Don had a dual sensory loss. Visual impairment and hearing impairment are each difficult to understand because of the innumerable manifestations a loss may exhibit. For the untrained or inexperienced, a total loss is more clearly understood. Seeing nothing is understandable; seeing some things sometimes, leads to confused notions of uncooperative behavior, laziness, stubbornness, etc. This applies to a hearing loss as well, which is clearly exemplified by the statement of Don's teachers that he could "hear when he wants to." Of course, Don having a dual sensory impairment presents an even more complex picture. The impact this dual loss has on language and on underlying concept formation provides a challenge for even trained and experienced individuals. And these are very few.

In order for individuals to work effectively with deaf-blind children and adults, it is essential to have an open spirit of communication. Professionals have some skills that may be put to use but they do not "know everything." Parents have a good deal of knowledge about their child, but they also do not "know everything." Then there is the deaf-blind individual who is, after all, the expert. It is only with the cooperative effort of everyone, uninfluenced by preconceived notions, that effective teaching or service may occur. If professionals believe they should be experts, they become threatened. If parents feel they know everything, they lose out on an objective viewpoint. The deaf-blind individual who has no control over his or her life, loses self-respect.

One of the problems that impedes open communication is that we tend to look at this moment. We fail to realize that everyone brings to a communicative interaction years of experience and a multiplicity of relationships. I believe professionals have been particularly at fault in not recognizing this. For example, the parents' relationship to Don includes the effect of having a daughter die at an early age of a congenital tumor. This undoubtedly contributes to the parents' stress. Professionals who base their interaction only on Don and his parents have missed an important contribution to interaction—the family unit.

Parents also may focus on the handicapped child rather than on the family unit. Don's mother points out the problem with Don's brother because so much of their effort was placed on Don. Parents need to realize that other members of the family, siblings, grandparents, etc., also have a valuable role in the family and are able to contribute to the well-being of the child with an impairment. Don's brother had the potential to provide Don with social skills; he held the ticket to greater peer acceptance. Siblings, in their rough and tumble style, provide the first experience in proving oneself competent in establishing a peer relationship. By focusing less on Don, his brother might have become an ally at an earlier age. In addition, the disabled child is forced to assume the burden of being responsible for taking from others in the family what rightfully belongs to them.

There is another interference in communication that I call the "crazies." Years ago, one of my children was tentatively diagnosed as having muscular dystrophy, and at another time, of being emotionally disturbed. Although both problems did not come to pass, I can still remember several months of being a "crazy woman." I can remember the anger I felt toward professionals, some of it justified, some of it not. People who came in contact with me, also met my anger that this was happening to someone I loved, my fears for the future, my frustrations because I could not "make it go away," my guilt because maybe I did something to cause the problem. I was not an easy person to deal with.

The parents of a young deaf-blind boy, Susan and Mike, and I have begun a Developmental Center for Deaf-Blind Children. The school, designed to give young deaf-blind children intensive early intervention, has from the very beginning of its conceptualization (the "wouldn't it be nice" if stage) viewed parents as a major force in the school's direction. Even so, we knew that in spite of our philosophy and lack of bureaucracy, we would have to work with parents who, under stress, make communication difficult. As Susan says, "Parents are not easy to get along with, look at me!" Susan is now on the opposite side of the fence, and she sees another point of view.

In my search for a summary or conclusion to the thoughts presented, I am led to the conviction that we all—deaf-blind child as well as adult, parents, professional, members of our society—must teach each other and learn from each other. We must learn freely and we must teach gently.

ANDERS

Anders was born on September 5, 1971. Suffering from Lebers congenital amaurose, he has been deaf-blind from his birth. Anders may be considered deaf and partially sighted, which means he has a very small sight ability, and for very short distances only. Although Anders' deaf blindness has an origin other than German measles (rubella), he certainly shares his disabilities and fate with other deaf-blind children.

From Anders' birth, his mother, Pirjo, and I have been working in various ways for his development and for his future possibilities in life. Our efforts have been performed in close cooperation with professionals within the framework of our family, within a group of parents of deaf-blind children, and in Danish society.

This story is a short and not at all complete presentation of some of the experiences we have gone through as a result of efforts during past 10 years. I am very pleased as a parent of a deaf-blind to have the opportunity to contribute to a book intended for parents who most certainly share something very special.

During his whole life, Anders has been lacking motivation, curiosity, and initiative, the reason for which is obvious, when it is realized that most motivation is gained through a childs' visual and hearing experience. As a direct result, Anders was for many years far behind in motoric development.

Being informed that further progress, including intellectual development, was very much dependent on motoric abilities, we spent much effort on physical training with Anders, in particular during his first 5 years. Great events in this period were when he was able to roll on the floor, sit by himself, stand without support, and later on when he took the first step on his own. Anders was 3½ years old when this latter event took place—a great day for us and for Anders.

Before reaching this stage of development Anders was moved around in the house in our arms being allowed to feel the walls, pictures, and furniture in order to give him, as much as possible, a first impression of his environment. From the day of his first step he has been able to move and gain experience inside the house. This gave him new information and curiosity, accelerating his intellectual development. It certainly meant a great deal to him when he realized his ability to find persons, and later on when he became able to ask for favours like food or bath by taking our hand and leading us to the respective places for these activities.

For many years Anders was very sensitive to changes in his daily life. Strange people were not accepted in our house nor abrupt changes in food or physical environment. Any change had to be introduced gradually and in very small steps. Even when taking this into consideration, the step from milk to mashed or sieved food as well as the next step to almost normal food required great efforts, ingenuity, and patience. Other situations also required great patience, like changing the environment in the eating situation, for example changing from bottle to cup, from being fed to handling a spoon or fork by himself, moving from one table to another, or changing from eating inside the house to eating outside. This dependence on a known environment and a known daily routine caused problems in connection with external relations which will be touched upon in a subsequent section.

Regarding sleeping habits, our first observation was that Anders when sleeping awaken by the most tiny vibration of his bed and that it was difficult keeping him asleep when moving him in the pram. Consequently, he often slept when he was not supposed to sleep and often he was awake most of the night, leaving the parents awake too, which resulted in all of us being almost continuously exhausted and irritated. Later on we learned that this sleeping pattern and the resulting problems are well-known by most parents of deaf-blind children. In addition to the psychological pressure, we also felt a severe physical load during this period. Assistance from the outside to provide relief was greatly needed.

For most children, play with toys contributes greatly to development. For Anders this road of development was very narrow. Lack of visual ability and concepts and, when in the baby age, great aversion to certain surfaces, especially soft surfaces and formless items, made him quite uninterested in playing with toys. He liked to carry and manipulate a favorite toy in his hands, however, in a nonconstructive or self-stimulating way. Self-stimulating activities like teeth grinding and eye poking were also practiced by Anders if he was left without being stimulated in other ways. Most parents know that even when providing a deaf-blind child with proper stimulation and activities, the way out of such unattractive self-stimulating activities may be long and difficult.

Anders was for many years very dependent on his daily life being firmly structured within the frame of a known environment in order to feel secure. Our goal then and now is development towards independence and as much as possible away from the need for such total security.

Another problem was toilet training, which like others, lasted for many years. This in itself is a step towards independence and also very much lightens daily work and the need for cleaning and washing. This made time and resources available for other more important work with Anders. In addition, this problem was associated with Anders' hanging on to old habits and systems and feeling insecure when exposed to changes. Anders, 11 years of age, now manages to go to the toilet by himself when needed, but still he needs subsequent assistance and at times still has accidents.

When Anders was one year old, we were for the first time instructed in how to start developing communication with Anders. We were told how to take the child's hand to his mouth to express food or eating and that it should always be done in close connection with the food or the eating situation. After five years, and after having done this hundreds and hundreds of times, Anders seemed to make the connection between the sign and its meaning so that he, in this way, could be told to come to eat at the usual place. Today he understands a limited number of signs and only on our firm request he may express himself by using a few signs, among which the sign for food is an important one. Without knowing it, by doing so he is rewarding us for all our efforts more than could be done in any other way.

Family Life

All parents have great expectations when looking forward to the arrival of a child. Parents of a deaf-blind child have the same expectations without having any presentiment of anything being wrong. In the case of Anders he was a very much wished-for child who had been carefully planned to arrive at a particular time in order for us to be able to provide him with the best possible starting conditions in life.

It was shocking, therefore, when we were informed that something was wrong with our child. It happened when Anders was 9 months old. For a long time we did not realize the problem and its consequences. Later on, it was a deep disappointment when we realized that none of our plans and dreams for our boy would ever come true. We asked with some bitterness ourselves, why should it happen to us; we felt it completely unjustified.

At that time we did not have much knowledge about any kind of handicap. Therefore, we highly needed qualified support and advice in order to understand what deaf-blindness and its consequences were and what possibilities may or may not exist for a deaf-blind child's development. After some time, we were gradually prepared to realize the situation and its consequences for our family. In time we were gradually able to accept this as an unescapable reality. This I believe is necessary if parents are to be suited to the great challenge of being parents to a deaf-blind child.

Having a deaf-blind child in the family changes family life in many ways, many of which involve potential problems. Parents in this situation and especially in the earliest stages have to meet and discover each other in a position completely unknown to either of them. Great conflicts may arise, the marriage may not stand the pressure and fall apart. On the other hand, the marriage may be strengthened.

During the period of having children, decisions regarding job and career often have to be made. In order for the family to have enough resources left for the deaf-blind child, it may be necessary to reduce career ambitions. It may even be necessary for one of the parents to give up job and career completely. I believe that most parents of deaf-blind children have had serious discussions on how to manage and how to distribute some home duties and the work with the child.

Relations Within the Environment

Taking the deaf blind child outside the home to see a medical specialist, to visit family elsewhere, visiting friends, doing shopping, etc. presents several problems. Anders was completely panicked when brought to a new and unknown environment and to strange people. In the beginning we were ashamed of the child, who behaved in a strange way with other people; the whole story of the child had to be explained over and over to everybody who saw him for the first time. Anders was not toilet-trained even when several years old. We had to bring lots of clothes for every possibility and also it was necessary to bring only the special food accepted by Anders. It has taken lots of physical as well as psychological effort to overcome such difficulties and problems when trying to integrate Anders into family life and into life outside the home.

Despite kindness and understanding from family and friends, neighbors and others, we have felt relief and benefitted substantially from meeting other parents of deaf-blind children for mutual exchange of experiences, support, and encouragement.

One of the risks of having a deaf-blind child in the family is that of the parents and child developing too much mutual dependence. The parents need to spend some time on their own without the child, to relax fully on a day or evening off, or on a vacation. Several problems exist, however, in getting a nurse qualified and willing to take the responsibility for a deaf-blind child even for a short period. For longer periods, like a vacation or a weekend, the possibility of care within a deaf-blind institution with professional personnel has been available to us. Even then it was difficult to leave a small deaf-blind boy to the care of others. However, there has been no other way for us to get relief, and to recharge ourselves with new energy and optimism for future work with Anders. In addition to this, it was at that time part of making Anders more independent.

Relations to Specialist and Advisers

The complex nature of the handicap of Anders has involved several medical specialists, all of whom have done an excellent job within their particular fields of specialization.

It is my general experience, however, that many medical experts within their respective professional fields concentrate exclusively on the child considering the case purely as a medical one, and not always paying attention to statements made by parents despite such statements being based on months of careful observations which could be of great relevance and importance in the clinical medical examination.

During all the various medical examinations, when we have taken Anders from one specialist to another, we have had hope that the next examination would indicate some medical solution to the problem. At the same time, we have feared that yet another disability might be discovered.

It has been disappointing to learn that even among specialists the knowledge of the multiple disability and the educational possibilities for deaf-blind children often is very limited. Usually reference is made to deaf or blind care or both, resulting in advisers from both disability groups arriving and giving different advice.

When we ultimately were referred to deaf-blind care, and were visited for the first time by a kind person, qualified and experienced in dealing with deaf-blind problems and expressing great understanding, then for the first time we felt that there was some hope, and some real possibilities for progress. We were fortunate to be in that position at an early stage, when Anders was not very much older than one year.

Anders at Present

Anders is now 11 years old. Since his fourth year he has attended the Deaf-Blind School in Aalborg, which is the only school for deaf-blind children in Denmark. As we live far from the school, Anders is living in a school home close to the school. However, every weekend and all school holidays, including 7 weeks in the summer, Anders is at home or travels with us in Denmark or abroad. Every Monday morning Anders has a 3-hour journey including half an hour by airplane from Copenhagen to Aalborg to reach his school and he repeats this journey Friday afternoon when he returns back home.

During the years Anders has made substantial progress in many ways. He has developed motorically to be relatively independent, if the ground is not too rough. He is almost able to dress himself and with some assistance he can manage toilet visits. Anders now enjoys any kind of food and new adventures at home or elsewhere. He still lacks initiative to engage himself to play with toys in a relevant manner. However, Anders has developed into a happy boy. He accepts his school and being away from us during the week, but every Friday when arriving at home his sunny face tells us, that after all he is most happy being at home together with his parents.

The Unknown Future

It is possible for Anders to continue at the Deaf-Blind School in Aalborg until he is 18 years old. From 18 to 23 years of age, Anders will be eligible to attend a newly established Institution for Deaf-Blind Youth in Aalborg. In this institution, emphasis is put on prevocational training and further training toward greatest possible independency.

We realize that Anders will never reach complete independence. As parents we are deeply concerned and feel responsibility for the quality of life available to Anders as a deaf-blind adult. Our joint efforts in this respect are effectively exerted through The Danish Deaf-Blind Association newly initiated by a group of parents of deaf-blind children in Denmark.

PSYCHOLOGICAL INTERPRETATION

Harry L. Dangel

The story of Anders and his parents provides a great deal of information for the reader to consider about the struggle of a family to raise and care for a deaf-blind child. One can examine their story from the perspective of analyzing what is unique about Anders and about the manner in which his parents coped with his development. To take this approach, however, risks making the experiences of this family isolated from the experiences of others. We learn from the lives of others because we can identify commonalities between their experiences and our own lives. It is most instructive to examine the story of Anders and his parents from the perspective of how Anders' development is a reflection of the development of other children and how his parents' frustrations and concerns follow patterns that are similar to those of other parents with handicapped children, and of parents in general. The uniqueness in the story of Anders and of his parents is that the steps of Anders development are so small that we seem to be viewing them through a powerful microscope that his parents' attempts to balance support and protection for Anders with developing independence for him are greatly intensified, and that the compromises of the parents in adjusting personal pleasures and ambitions to accomodate family demands are extended to the extremes.

Anders father describes Anders road of development as being "very narrow." It is an appropriate and accurate description. As with any child, the initial periods of learning for Anders were very inefficient. The exploring, testing, and confirming of the self as related to the environment, a critical foundation for later development in all children was magnified and greatly extended. His parents role in providing varied physical experiences was a crucial step in developing the basis for subsequent development, but for Anders the time table was written in years rather than months. Anders lack of curiosity and iniative, his need for structure

60

and consistency and slowness in toilet training were areas of development that concerned his father. Although Anders father expressed awareness that Anders handicap explained the lack of initiative, the father's concerns suggest a continuing frustration over Anders slow progress.

Anders slowness in the areas of initiative and exploring, dressing, and toileting might be explained using a developmental model of needs such as proposed by Maslow. Maslow states that a hierarchy of needs exists and that needs at the lowest levels must be met before an individual will seek to meet higher level needs. The lowest level of needs proposed are physiological, for example, hunger and thirst. These needs were obviously amply provided. It is at the next level, the safety needs (i.e., stability, security, and order), that a deaf-blind child such as Anders is vulnerable. The nature of Anders handicap is such that providing assurance of stability security and order for him is a lengthy process. Furniture must consistently be in the same location, food must be the same, schedules the same for a long time in order to provide the level of predictability needed to meet Anders safety needs. Until safety needs are met, Maslow would suggest that Anders would be expected to be relatively unresponsive to having any higher needs met. These higher level needs would include the affection and social praise that accompany toilet training, dressing, and other areas of self-help skills. Anders development, when viewed from this perspective, is seen as similar to the patterns of other children but, because of his handicap, is greatly delayed. This is especially true for any area of development dependent upon higher level reinforcers such as social praise.

There is a sense of parental isolation that runs throughout Anders father's story that parallels Anders own isolation. Much of the struggle faced by the parents of deaf-blind children involves balancing the family's needs for mutual dependence and the isolation from others which provides protection and safety with the risk that parents and Anders face in being involved with others and ultimately more independent. The pull toward isolation is powered by the awareness that, although family and friends wish to understand, only those parents with similar experiences can provide mutual support and encouragement. The risk of public embarrassment because of Ander's strange behavior, the awareness that psysicians typically do not have the experience or the inclination to deal with the combination of physical and emotional problems which accompany a deaf-blind handicap, and the concern that something might happen to Anders if the parents leave him in the care of another are all strong factors which promote family isolation.

Fortunately for Anders and his parents there were supportive resources available to overcome the isolation. The primary supportive resource is, of course, the relationship between the parents. Anders father alludes to the conflicts and pressures upon the marriage of parents of a deaf-blind child. The father insightfully describes discovering one's mate in a situation that is "completely unknown to either of them" and of the risks to the marriage that must be overcome. It was necessary for each parent to overcome the desire to separate oneself from the family, to deal with whatever feelings of guilt or anger that might exist and develop a renewed relationship with one's mate. He describes the conflict between the need he and his wife had to spend time together to replenish their emotional resources and the need to always be with Anders. On a broader level, there were the resources of the community—a person to instruct them in how to communicate with Anders starting at age one, the parents of other deaf-blind children with whom to share experiences, and a deaf-blind institute to which Anders could be sent. Anders story shows a clear pattern of parents learning to accept risks to in order to overcome isolation for both Anders and themselves. It also emphasizes the importance of various layers of support, beginning with the family, then of friends and acquaintences, and finally of the level of society's commitment to the handicapped in helping the family to overcome their isolation.

There is a note of intellectual stoicism in the manner in which Anders' father tells his story. The message is often not only what is said, but also what is not said. The condition which caused Anders' blindness, Lebers congenital amaurose, is a genetically-transmitted handicap. As such, there are possible consequences that any other children that Anders' parents might have had would have been born with the same condition. There is no discussion in the story about this factor or about any difficulty the parents had in accepting that Anders would be this couple's only child. In a detached manner, Anders' father describes the possibility that parents with a child such as Anders may need to reduce career ambitions without stating that this has occurred or the parents reaction to modifying their career ambitions. He states that marriages may stay together or fall apart, but he does not directly describe his own marriage. The reader can only assume that Anders' parents learned to adjust their relationship to accomodate the new demands that were placed on them by the birth of their son. Anders' father speaks of physicians who view his son's problems from a limited medical orientation and yet, expressed no anger or frustration at the physicians. The reader can only imagine the parents' disappointment at receiving so little information and support from the professionals who were probably seen as providing the only hope for overcoming Anders' handicap.

JULIE

Father's Statement

Our financial status was a great problem the first five years of Julie's life. My wife was not able to work while she was caring for Julie and taking her to the Kennedy Center in Nashville. Julie was ill very often during those years. We have a very good medical insurance coverage where I am employed, but even that would not pay all the bills.

We paid for all of the mileage and tuition at the Kennedy Center. We traveled approximately 120 miles per day, four days per week, until she was four years of age. At age four the school system began to pay for the mileage and tuition. During this time we had "worn out" two cars, both with over 100,000 miles when traded.

Sandra had her hands full with Julie and I could not have survived without her. I worked three and four jobs those first years, maintaining my regular full-time daily job and selling vacuum cleaners at night. Each Sunday I ran a paper route and on some Saturdays, I worked at a local service station.

When Julie was born, we had accumulated approximately $1,100 but this was very quickly used up. The costs mounted and we have never been able to catch up. We are doing better now, however, and I sincerely hope that trend continues.

Depression was a big factor those first years and I feel my personality changed during this time. I felt sorry for myself and for Julie. I would feel guilty if Sandra and I even went out to dinner. I would be thinking Julie was home possibly in pain or not being able to breathe properly.

The Child Study Center at Peabody College played a big part in helping us with our depression and guilt feelings. They conducted studies on Julie and us in 1974, 1976, and 1978. Just talking to someone who understands and takes time to listen helped us a great deal.

Occasionally, there is still some depression; however, we are now handling the situation very well. We are happy at this time and appreciate all the blessings Julie has brought into our lives.

Mother's Statement

Our daughter Julie was born with multiple birth defects. She had a cleft lip and palate, deformed left ear, heart disease, was severely mentally retarded, and legally blind-deaf.

Julie has been in the hospital 12 times since birth. She has had her cleft lip and palate repaired and her pulmonary artery banded. She still has a heart problem, but will not require surgery unless her health starts to deteriorate. Generally, Julie is doing very well these days.

At fourteen months of age, a doctor at Vanderbilt Hospital advised us to take Julie to the John F. Kennedy Center at George Peabody College in Nashville, Tennessee. The Kennedy Center is an experimental school and a child study center.

Julie was evaluated by the Multiple Handicap Evaluation Team to evaluate progress made and to determine appropriate educational programming. It was at their suggestion that we enrolled her in the John F. Kennedy Center. This was one of the most important things we did for Julie, and for us too. The Kennedy Center worked with Julie and instructed us, as parents, in how to work with her also.

Julie was so small and fragile. At 14 months of age, she only weighed about 15 pounds and could not sit up or crawl. I did not work at that time. My entire life was built around my little baby girl and keeping her alive. We never had a full night's sleep. We had to get up at intervals and suction her. She was sick constantly and was running a high temperature. She had pneumonia often and would go into congestive heart failure.

As I spent more time with her, I wanted to teach her everything possible. She was our first child and, with all her problems, how could I do it? Julie would not let me hold and cuddle her. She wanted only to sit in her carryall or lie flat on her back in her crib, but we kept every kind of stimulant toy over her crib and around her, and we always talked to her. She would laugh and "what a beautiful laugh it was!" Everything, no matter how small, was so important.

Julie, now a very happy and somewhat healthy young lady who has just celebrated her twelfth birthday, enjoys playing with her sister Jeanie (age 7) and her brother Kenny (age 5). They too, even as children, have learned and accepted, and are very proud of their handicapped sister. Julie is always included and is always made to feel a part of our family. She attends Sunday school and church each week with the rest of the family. She loves to travel and has gone with us to Florida on three different occasions for vacation.

Julie continues to make progress and so do we as parents. She has learned to communicate using sign language, not only with us, but with her teacher and baby sitters. If they don't understand her, then sister Jeanie is always there to help. Jeanie too knows the signs and is very proud of her knowledge.

Without the support of Julie's maternal grandparents, she could not have made her remarkable progress. Through most of Julie's life we could not use babysitters and we had to depend solely on my family. My mother and father were always there when we needed someone to turn to.

Our pediatrician gave us little hope. He was very frank and told us that our child would only be a vegetable and that she would never sit up, walk, or talk. It was very hard to listen to the doctor say these things, but we thought there was still hope and we would not give up. Our hope came from the small things that Julie did. As an example, Julie was so observant. She would watch me manicure my nails and then she would try to do her nails. Our pediatrician did not consider these little things Julie did as being that important, but nevertheless, he decided to send Julie to Kennedy Center for testing at Peabody College. She tested in the severely retarded area, but the staff was fascinated with the way in which Julie would imitate us. If we would place our hands on top of our heads, she would also do this. Everything we could do with our hands, she would do while sitting in her little carry-all. So, they asked us if we would bring her to school four days per week to attend their morning program. We knew the expense involved just for the trip alone (60 miles one way), but we were so excited and we agreed.

Starting Julie in this program was the turn-around in all our lives. We learned so much, not from just the teacher, but from all the other parents. We were like one big family. We had a mutual problem and we combined our thoughts to solve it. One of the parents told us how she had taught her child to feed herself by standing behind the child and going through every movement with her hand on top of the child's hand.

Everything Julie learned was slow and it took a considerable amount of time and patience as everything had to be learned in stages. The smallest task would have to be broken down into several parts. Soon I could sit beside her and just put my hand on hers and she would start the food to her mouth; then I would drop my hand and she would proceed.

Then it came to the point where all I had to do was put the food on the spoon and she would put it in her mouth. Eventually, she could feed herself without help.

Learning to walk was the same. The teacher would design a program for her to work on while she was at the Kennedy Center. We were involved because the teachers would start a task and we had to carry it out at home. We worked with Julie in the classroom while being observed by the teachers. They would instruct us in how to carry out the program at home. They let us take parallel bars home to help with Julie's walking. Several times a day we would stand and move her hands and feet alternately. Julie got so she loved to walk down the bars by herself. I think she knew she was showing off. Julie would hold on to my finger or to a stick and would walk everywhere, but she would not walk alone. It was so frustrating. About this time, I became pregnant with Jeanie and I so wanted Julie to walk. About two weeks before Jeanie was born, Julie just turned loose and started walking. I will never forget that moment and how I thought other parents take this for granted. But our joy was short-lived. Julie suddenly became very ill and had to go to the hospital. While there she had a high temperature and developed congestive heart failure. It was as if she were in a coma; she just lay there. Our family doctor came in early the next morning and told us Julie would not live and that she had done all she could, but that Julie's heart was terribly weak. Well, I cried and the doctor sat with me for about an hour until my husband Ken arrived. The next morning came and Julie was awake playing and sitting up in bed. She ate the biggest breakfast. This was not the first time that we had been told that Julie would not make it, so we constantly live with the realization that death could come at any time.

About a week later, Jeanie was born, a beautiful, healthy baby girl. It took Julie six months to learn to walk again, but we never gave up no matter how great the odds were against us.

By this time our pediatrician had retired. During my last visit with him, he called me into his office and told me that I had taught him something that in all his years in practice he had never learned, and that was to never give up on children such as Julie. He said that if she had been born to anyone else, she would never have walked or learned all the things she had learned, but that I could not accept all the credit. Without the people at the Kennedy Center, it would not have been possible. He said he hoped that I would have other children someday.

My husband and I had a study done at Vanderbilt that showed that

Julie had all her genes and chromosomes and that it was safe for us to have other children.

Currently, Julie continues to become stronger and has developed in ways that no one could ever have imagined were possible. Julie was potty-trained before she could walk and knew all her shapes and colors. However, she has never learned to speak, although she would laugh and cry. We thought there might be a hearing problem; however, she has been tested several times at the Bill Wilkerson Hearing & Speech Center with always the same results—hearing in the lower limits of the normal level.

Starting Julie's education at 15 months of age, really helped her to get a head start. We believe that had Julie not gone to the Kennedy Center, she would have been bedridden her entire life. The 5 ½ years of training not only helped her, but helped us in teaching Julie and in accepting her handicap.

Julie is presently enrolled in the Special Education Class at Eastside School in Shelbyville, Tennessee. We feel Julie could do better in the schools in Nashville, but this is not possible. Our school system has come a long way in special education in the last five years. There is much more they could do if the monies were available, but we accept what they are doing.

We want to thank all the people that have helped in any way with Julie's education. The Southeast Regional Deaf-Blind Center has helped in many ways and we appreciate it. The Parent-Teacher Workshops that the Southeastern Regional Deaf-Blind Center has sponsored have really helped tremendously. We have been able to attend four of these workshops and it is always good to be able to talk to other parents with problems similar to ours. They always seem to know and understand how we feel. Additionally, most of the teachers and other professional people dealing with the handicapped have helped us in dealing with our problems.

PSYCHOLOGICAL INTERPRETATION

Paul D. Cotton

First, I would like to thank both of these parents for their willingness to share—both parents and workers in the field—the feelings and experiences they have had and continue to have as a result of having a child who is multi-handicapped. I was particularly pleased that the father responded as very little is known of the feelings of fathers of children with handicapping conditions. This is partially due to the fact that men in our society are not supposed to be "emotional" but rather are expected to "be strong" and support the wife. Hopefully, such an attitude is changing.

The awareness of other services by one of the physicians was quite exciting. The physician did not know what to do but did know someone who might be willing to help and know how to help in the training of their child. The first physician's attitude is still too prevalent, so it was a pleasure to read of the other physician's approach. This points out the need for workshops to train physicians and other people representing various disciplines which impact the family and child, if not directly, at least peripherally. We must all be aware of our professional strengths and deficits not using them as an excuse not to know other resources within our area and state.

In the mother's report, she emphasized the extreme importance of parents being referred to services early in the life of the child. This helped them not only to be able to be involved in the training of their child while they were still optimistic about the child's ability to develop but also has helped them to be more aware of their child's condition and thus helped in accepting their child. It is important for parents to be "realistic optimists," i.e., being aware of the deficits of their child and also knowing how to utilize the strengths of their child to help compensate for some of the weaknesses. The old song, "You've Got to Accentuate the Positive, Eliminate the Negative, Latch on to the Affirmative" is so appropriate in being involved with children such as their child. When "acceptance" is discussed, the goal is to have a positive acceptance of being aware that the child will not be able to accomplish all of the tasks a nonhandicapped child might be able to accomplish while at the same time guarding against a negative or fatalistic acceptance. The interpretation of "God's Will" has done much to foster a negative acceptance.

The comments pertaining to the importance of an extended family to help is most important. The fact that the parents would utilize members of the extended family is positive. Too often parents of handicapped children are hesitant to utilize such even when it is available and is offered. They perceive it as "their responsibility" to care for the child. The father did mention that at times when they took time for themselves there was some guilt produced. It is most important that the couple, of particularly a handicapped child, be aware that time spent with each other, alone, is an important factor that can help them cope with being the parents. In talking with parents, I recommend at least one night a week out. When the question of finances comes up, I say that if they can't afford to have a babysitter and go to a movie that they have a babysitter and go sit in the car for at least two hours so that communication does not break down between the two of them.

It is to the advantage of the entire family that all are not involved in outings. The acceptance of the other children of the handicapped child is directly indicative of the acceptance of this child by the parents. This is an area which needs to be addressed by professionals in the field. Fortunately, we are becoming more aware that not only do children with handicapping conditions have fathers, but they are also part of a network including siblings.

The father's comments pertaining to feelings of depression and guilt are quite honest and realistic being very unusual for a male. Certainly during the nine months the mother was carrying the child there was probably little or no thought that the child would be handicapped. When we get what we are not expecting there is always disappointment unless it is a pleasant surprise and if the disappointment is because of our child then there is inherent a sense of guilt because we are not supposed to feel this way toward our own child—so we think. There is some support to the notion that before we can accept the "real" child, the "ideal" child must die so that the amount of conflict between the "real" and the "ideal" will be gone. At times you hear parents of children with handicapping conditions say, "If Tom were not deaf-blind, at 21 he would be doing such and such." This is wishful thinking and lack of a positive acceptance of the realities of life. At 21, Tom could be in prison for multiple murders. We never know.

With financial concerns the family was experiencing, there was cause for frustration and many other emotions that are understandable but also produce some guilt for the parent as where our child is concerned we are to think that no cost is too much.

As the father says, they are doing pretty well now and being able to cope with situations that arise. There will be other times in their lives when situations present themselves which will conjure up these same feelings of depression and guilt. Two things are in their favor at such times. One is that they admit such feelings and thus are able to talk about them and seek assistance in dealing with them. The other is that they have had them before and have successfully coped with them so that they have a history of successful coping upon which to build.

One of the most important comments both parents made was the necessity of having people who were willing to take the time to "listen" to them. This is probably one of the major faults of people with professional training in the helping professions. Quite often we are so busy helping that we don't stop and listen to the requests being made of us. If we are to be of maximum assistance to the family, then we must always stop and listen before we proceed. Not only must we listen to the words that are being said, but also to feelings and to what is being said nonverbally. Again, this is not saying that the teacher or whoever is the primary worker with the child and family must be "all things to all people." We must also know where we need to refer to someone else and to whom we should refer this couple. Perhaps the phrase, "Stop, Look, and Listen Before We Talk," might be quite appropriate for we folks with training and interest in helping parents help themselves and their family grow.

Not only did they emphasize the importance of professionals who would listen, they also emphasized the importance of having the opportunity to talk with other parents who had or were experiencing many of the same feelings, problems, and concerns as they had. Hopefully, such opportunities will be able to be continued.

In summary, it was my pleasure to have the opportunity to visit briefly in the lives of this couple and their family. The importance of us as professionals knowing resources available and how to access such, to stop and listen to parents and to incorporate them as a members of the team working with their child, and how to help support their own growth through this experience was emphasized. As stated in the beginning, I appreciate their willingness to share honestly and openly. I hope to meet this couple and their family some day.

LAURENCE

Laurence was born September 20, 1973, weighing 6 lb 6 oz. My husband, Phillip, and I had no inkling of there being anything abnormal about him, and neither did the doctors—at first. By about three days he was severely jaundiced and was placed under an ultraviolet light in the neonatal ward of the maternity hospital, but as this was not particularly unusual, we were not unduly concerned. When Laurence was six days old, he was given the standard checkover before being discharged, and we were given our first real shock—Laurence had noises in his heart that startled the doctors and they wanted him to be seen by a specialist in this field before he came home. Because my bed was needed for another patient, and I was in good health, I was sent home without my new baby and we were to call back next day to talk to the specialist after he had examined Laurence. After waiting for about three hours the specialist appeared and told us that the valves in Laurence's heart were not working efficiently and that he wanted to do a thorough examination at the cardiac out-patient's clinic, in about three weeks time, but for now we could take our baby home.

Home we all went, and began our troubles of trying to feed a baby who only wanted to scream and kick and fight. As a brand new mother who had never had any experience with babies, I had no idea how babies normally behave. If Laurence had been our second or third child we would have been very worried about our very active baby who cried constantly, but as they say, ignorance is bliss.

By the time Laurence was three weeks old, our local general practitioner was sufficiently concerned by the slow weight gain, to have Laurence admitted to Karitane Hospital (a local hospital which specializes in the care of babies). After a few days he was examined by the visiting pediatrician who telephoned to ask Phillip and I to go and see her as soon as possible. We went straight over and after another long wait, Phillip had to go back to work. Shortly after he had left, I was called in to the office and told conversationally, "Did you know your baby has cataracts?". I was totally stunned. In his short life Laurence had been seen by numerous doctors and nurses and there had been no suggestion of any further problems. The bad news was not over yet. The pediatrician then asked me if I had any spots on my skin in the early stages of my pregnancy and I recalled that I had indeed had an itchy rash only a few days after having had my pregnancy diagnosed. At the time, I had gone to my local doctor regarding the rash and had been told that it was just a nervous rash due to the excitement of having found I was pregnant. The doctor did not do any tests to check this theory and I did not question the diagnosis. I was told to buy some calamine lotion to soothe the rash. I never gave it another thought. The pediatrician listened to this and then said that she thought it very likely that my "nervous rash" was in fact rubella. She said that she wanted Laurence to be transferred to Auckland Hospital so that thorough tests could be done to confirm this. While I waited for the ambulance that had been ordered for us, I then had to ring Phillip at the local public telephone box and tell him the news. He was very disappointed and concerned. At Auckland Hospital, Laurence began a series of tests, and after having had blood samples taken, I was told I could go home. When the results came through, we were told that by a comparative study of the levels of rubella antibodies in my blood and Laurence's, they could confirm that it was definitely rubella that I had had in those early weeks. Next came an explanation of the implications of this: that Laurence was possibly affected in his hearing and could be brain damaged as well. We were told that every cell in his body had been affected, and he would be small and would not develop at the normal rate, and would never achieve a normal level of ability. After about ten days, Laurence came home again, after the doctors were satisfied that he had gained a little more weight.

At eight weeks we returned to Greenlane Hospital to the cardiac unit for another check on his heart. They were so anxious about his failure to thrive that they kept him there, initially for observation. We lived very close to this hospital at the time, and I had walked there with Laurence in the pram as it was a lovely sunny day. For me, one of the lowest times in my life was walking home with an empty pram, with dear old ladies coming up to smile at a nonexistent baby. That Sunday, we had Laurence christened in the hospital, with our vicar, the god-parents and us all wearing white gowns and masks, while our families watched through the glass from the corridor. These precautions were to reduce the risk of infection to this poor little scrap of life who was in no condition to fight.

A few days later the surgeons performed an exploratory operation to ascertain the precise nature of the faults with Laurence's heart. Apart from sundry relatively minor problems, Laurence had a condition called patent ductus arteriosis. As an unborn baby does not use it's lungs at all, the circulatory system by-passes the lungs with a blood vessel, and shortly after birth this vessel closes so that all the blood goes around the lungs. This did not happen in Laurence's case and his blood was not being oxygenated properly. At ten weeks old this vessel was closed surgically, after we had been informed by the surgeon that Laurence had a fifty-fifty chance of coming out of surgery alive. He survived, broke all records with his swift recovery, and came home just in time for Christmas. Laurence was now three months old, had spent only five weeks at home and had been in three different hospitals, not counting the maternity hospital where he was born.

Life now settled down with a routine of check-ups with all of the different doctors and specialists who had seen Laurence. At one of these I was told that Laurence should really be put in an institution as he would be a vegetable all of his life. We disregarded that advice as we felt it ridiculous to write-off someone's entire life on the basis of their achievements at a few weeks old. We felt that if we put a lot of work into stimulating him and giving him every chance we could to help his development, then he was very likely to exceed the expectations of the pessimistic experts around us. Looking back now, we were very naive, but our faith was not misplaced, and if we had not been so determined to "show them," Laurence would probably have vegetated until he *did* become a vegetable, a rather interesting case of the chicken or the egg coming first.

At five months, Laurence had his first hearing tests at the National Audiology Center. These turned out to be a complete waste of time as Laurence was totally uncooperative, but they did not feel he was totally deaf. At five and a half months, Laurence had the first of what was to be eight small eye operations, each involving a stay in hospital of about five days. These were to remove the cataracts in both eyes.

Through the months ahead, Laurence was very slow with his milestones and continued to make only poor weight gains. During this period, each day (and night) was difficult and we survived on a philosophy of taking one day at a time and only trying to cope with that day's problems.

When Laurence was eighteen months old we had our next major

disaster—meningitis. One day I went to check him in his cot as it was time for his next meal, and he was lying very still with his eyes open, and I was sure something was very wrong. It was the weekend, and I called to Phillip to come and have a look. In the few moments that we stood beside him, he started to froth at the mouth and went into convulsions. We raced with him in the car to the local doctor, who after a quick check telephoned Auckland Hospital to say we were on our way. Laurence appeared to me to be deteriorating fast and I thought I may have to give him "mouth to mouth" to get him there. The relief when we arrived at the hospital, where there was oxygen and doctors, was tremendous. The emergency team in the children's wing swung into action to bring down his temperature which was apparently very high, and they gave him a lumbar puncture and began a series of tests to determine the cause of these symptoms. Meningitis was confirmed. After a two-week stay in hospital, he was discharged and we quickly discovered that he was a very different boy from the one of only a few weeks before. He had reverted to babyhood, and wanted only to drink milk (out of a bottle) and sleep and lie awake in his cot. When I put him on the floor to play with lots of toys around him, he just screamed. We had to start all over again. It took about six months before he reached his premeningitus stage again, and even then we felt that he was less responsive to sound.

Around this time, at about two years old, I began taking him into the Crippled Children's Society for speech therapy and swimming. He made no headway at all with the speech therapy, but he adored the warm water at swimming. He laughed and splashed and was a joy to behold. We went in once a week for a year and it was always the bright spot of his week.

When he was three, we began going to the Deaf-Blind Unit at Homai College in Auckland. I took him two days per week, staying with him the whole time. It was an enormous relief being able to share the daily struggle with experienced staff who had been through it all many times before, and their expertise was a very real practical help. At four, he began going for two full days and three half days, traveling in the mornings on the school bus, and I collected him at midday on the half days. I clearly remember the first day that the Homai minibus came to collect him—I came back inside and skipped through the house—it felt so wonderful to be released from my responsibilities for a few hours. By now, I was only going out there for one day per week, the day that they all went out on a trip somewhere.

In July 1978, when Laurence was nearly five, he began being a weekly boarder. He still is, and enjoys having two homes. When he was younger he used to go to a "normal" kindergarten that is close to Homai College. His teacher took him and stayed with him, to help him get used to the society of other children, as the deaf-blind children did not take much notice of each other. During the time he has been at Homai College he has been introduced to Total Communication and Laurence has at last made contact with the world.

Problems in Finding Educational Placement

In the first few years we never worried at all about educational placement for Laurence—our "worriers" were too busy with a myriad of immediate problems! We were visited by a field officer from the Crippled Children Society, a physiotherapist from the Extra-Mural Hospital, an Advisor for the Deaf, as well as keeping in regular contact with the various specialized medical personnel, and with so many agencies overseeing our "case" we were confident that when he was about five (the usual school age in New Zealand) there would be somewhere for him to attend. It had not occurred to me that he could have a preschool education as well.

When Laurence was two years and nine months, I contacted the Royal New Zealand Foundation for the Blind after being advised to do so by the physiotherapist. A field officer came out to our house to meet Laurence and to fill out the usual screeds of forms. She asked if I would like Laurence to go to Homai College, which is the only school in New Zealand for blind children. I was amazed because I had assumed that Laurence was too badly handicapped to have even a remote chance of going there. For the first time I heard about the existence of a Deaf-Blind Unit there and was assured that Laurence was no worse than some of the other children. The field officer arranged a date for me to take Laurence out to the unit (only about a twenty minute drive from our house) for him to be assessed. We spent the day there, talking to the staff and being shown around the school, and for the first time I saw other deaf-blind children.

The visiting psychologist who assessed Laurence said that he wanted Laurence to begin attending the unit as soon as all the "red tape" could be processed, which was around his third birthday. At this age, Laurence was just beginning to walk, he had had no toilet training and was still in napkins, he drank from a bottle, ate only mushy sweet solids, e.g., custard, and only made animal-like grunts. He did however, show a very lively interest in everything around him and was on the "go" for much of the time. He did not have an afternoon nap and was a very lively child.

If we had joined the Foundation for the Blind at an earlier date, he would have been assessed earlier and recommendations made for a program for me to follow at home, with visits from a field officer. We would also have known about the existence of the Deaf-Blind Unit and would have seen for ourselves that it was the ideal place for Laurence.

Problems Created in Family Unit

We have been most fortunate in that our marriage has weathered the storms created by Laurence, and Phillip and I are very close, but we do know many others for whom a handicapped child has been the last straw. I have borne the brunt of the strain simply because I stay at home and have of necessity spent a tremendous amount of time with Laurence, whereas Phillip is self-employed and has always had to work long hours and so has not had as much contact with him. He has, however, always given me total moral support and has helped me as much as he could, given the demanding nature of his business. We have also been lucky in having a very supportive family who have helped with baby-sitting and given encouragement and have generally rallied round whenever a new crisis has arisen.

There is no question that having a handicapped child does make appalling demands on the rest of the family. Laurence being our first child meant that I was free to devote a lot of time to play with him and work on his problems. In the early years one of our major problems was simply lack of sleep. Because of his puny size, he needed night feeding for almost a year, and after that he simply wanted to play if he awoke in the night. It must have been about three years before we had an unbroken night's sleep, which does not improve one's disposition! Until he was about six, each meal entailed a lot of time also, as I had to prepare special foods for him and then I often had to force it down him, much of it going over me and him, which meant changes of clothes all around.

There was also a lot of frustration at having so little success and when there were long periods of time with no progress at all, we were anxious that he had reached the limit of his potential. When "normal" children go through a stage, one is always confident in the knowledge that they will come out of it, but with handicapped children, one has no way of knowing if it is in fact just a "stage they are going through" or if it is the way things are going to be for the rest of the child's life.

Because of Laurence's problems we waited a long time before we decided to have another child. Laurence was five years old and was settled at Homai as a weekly boarder when Jeremy arrived, so that weekends were the main stress periods. From the very day that Jeremy was born we found him completely different to our previous experience with babies. Every contact with him was joy and a delight and we at last discovered how babies should behave and, as we watched the unfolding miracle of Jeremy's development, we realized how very handicapped Laurence was. Every little thing had to be taught to Laurence slowly, painfully, and seemingly endlessly, whereas Jeremy learned quickly and effortlessly, largely by observation and imitation, which was of course a method not within the scope of a deaf-blind child. When Jeremy was nearly three years old we had a daughter, Sarah, and she is now fifteen months old. Laurence has at last learned that other people have rights, although he still walks over Sarah at times! Until we had the other two children, Laurence had had very little contact with normal children, and it has been very good for him to interact with children and not just adults. Laurence and Jeremy chase each other and will sit side by side building fancy block structures together. Laurence is highly amused at the prespeech noises that Sarah makes, but otherwise is not particularly interested in her, but this will probably change when Sarah is old enough to force him to take some notice of her by swiping his toys.

We noticed that Jeremy was very shy with other children, although he is very outgoing when amongst people he knows, and we concluded that with having a handicapped brother who behaves differently he was not sure how normal children behave. If we were at a park and he was half-way up the ladder at a slide and another child began to climb up behind him, he became upset and tried to climb down again without taking his turn. To help this situation, we enrolled him at a local preschool center and for the last year he has attended for two mornings a week, and he is now developing confidence in his play with other children. We do not expect that Sarah will have the same problem, as she will have Jeremy for an example and will plainly be able to distinguish between the behavior of handicapped and normal children.

Life is very busy with two young children and one handicapped one, and I find that I do not get any spare time to continue learning sign language at the class at Homai as I used to before Sarah's arrival. I am very glad that we let Laurence have a good start before having other children, because I would not have been able to give him the time and attention that he needed and I would probably have been too frazzled to get such tremendous enjoyment and satisfaction out of Jeremy. I also consider it most important to have other children, to regain one's sense of proportion and in order to have a relatively normal family life. It is all too easy to have the parents' lives completely revolve around the handicapped child, but having normal children who also have needs, restores the balance, and the handicapped member of the family takes his or her place as simply that, one member of the family.

Present Placement and Functioning

Laurence is currently attending the Deaf-Blind Unit at Homai College, where he has been since aged three. He is now nine years old. The unit has four trained teachers, one of whom is the head teacher, two teacher aids, and eight pupils, so there is an excellent pupil/teacher ratio. Laurence's teacher has one other pupil, but the head teacher also works with him, so he receives a great deal of individual attention.

The program has a lot of emphasis on physical development as the head teacher believes a healthy, stimulated body helps intellectual progress, and the children are certainly kept busy and fit. Every day they work in the gymnasium for half an hour, they have four hours swimming per week in the school's excellent indoor pool, and some of the children (Laurence among them) attend horse-riding for one hour each week at Riding for the Disabled—the other children who are not interested in the horse-riding going to Industrial Skills. Each week they have music sessions (percussion instruments, folk dancing, etc.), they have recently begun going roller skating (surprisingly successful!), and each week they all go on an outing to a place related to the current theme (e.g. if they are studying transport they go on train rides, bus rides, ferry rides, trip to the Museum of Transport and Technology, etc.). Some of the children (including Laurence) go on a shopping trip for an hour each week in order to teach them how to behave when out with their parents. They also do cooking each week (Laurence thoroughly enjoys the end products!), arts and crafts, six sessions of pottery in each of the three terms, and the children also help do the gardening in the flower beds around the unit. Each day Laurence has two individual work sessions, each fifteen minutes long, one with his teacher and one with the head teacher, when they work in a small private room on opposite sides of a small desk and require his undivided attention. In these sessions he does such work as:

signing the object in a picture, matching pictures, selecting the big or small airplane, etc. when asked, recognizing numbers up to three (how many boats, etc.), and matching objects with pictures. All of this is done in Total Communication, in Laurence's case signing and the teachers signing and talking. He is also taught to pattern with his speech noises, e.g., teacher goes "ah,ahhhh,ahhh," and Laurence has to copy. Each week he goes to the local normal primary school for one hour with a teacher aid where he joins a class of five six-year-old children. He enjoys these sessions and the children reportedly love having him in their class.

When preparing to write this, I asked his teacher to note down exactly what he is doing at present and this is what she records:

Receptive Language:	Labels 30–50 objects on request. Watches and imitates signs with increasing interest. Under— Understands simple "What," "Where" questions.
Expressive Language:	Will sometimes put 3+ words together (in signs), e.g., "Help me please," "Yellow arm bands" (at swimming time). He will ask for things he wants.
Gross Motor:	Loves swimming—head under water, kicks holding onto float board. Enjoys horse riding—stands in stirrups, mounts and dismounts, touches parts of the horse and unaided, participates in exercises. Trampoline—enjoys jumps, and sit-jumps.
Fine Motor:	Can string beads. Can complete a 10 piece puzzle. Holds a crayon—makes vertical, horizontal, and circular strokes.
Pre-Academic:	Can associate objects with pictures. Will concentrate in Individual Sessions for 20–30 minutes.
Socialization:	Initiates affectionate behavior with adults. Attends to and cooperates with adult-initiated play. Helps with tasks when asked to. Aware of different people. Shows initiative, e.g., will sign "toilet" and then disappear off to the swing!
Self-Care:	Can dress and undress. Enjoys most foods. Toilets himself.

Functioning Level:	Somewhere in the 4–5 year level (tested on Vineland Social Maturity Scale).
Communication:	18 months – 2 year developmental level.
Hearing:	Laurence has a 50–60 decibel loss binaurally in (at least) the 1–4 kHz region, with the left ear being a little worse than the right. (Laurence wears a hearing aid.)
Vision:	Aphakia – both eyes. (No lenses due to cataract removal.) Right eye – retina damaged (rubella), vision cloudy and fluctuating. Left eye – only light/dark differentiation. (Laurence wears glasses.)

Considering how little vision he has, it is remarkable the way he moves around. In a familiar environment such as home, he scarcely appears to have much vision loss, but if we go to a strange place he walks around carefully and checks everything very closely. He has no distance vision and cannot recognize people at more than about four meters. The Homai complex is laid out over a large area with paths connecting all the different blocks. If he is signed and told "Go to the hostel" he will do so independently. At home, the effect of his visual handicap is to limit him only in reading books (although he shows increasing interest in looking at pictures voluntarily) and watching television, as he can see well enough for playing with toys. He has a very natural-sounding and infectious laugh which provides a ready indication as to his opinion of activities – he always makes his opinions known one way or another! Laurence uses the Australian Victorian Sign System and although some of his signs are indistinct, he can basically make his wants and needs known. He will also sign with Jeremy and responds to Jeremy's signing, e.g., I can ask Jeremy to find Laurence and sign "biscuit and drink" and Laurence arrives on the run!

As a weekly boarder at Homai College, he is collected on Monday mornings in the school mini-bus and is delivered back at the house on Friday afternoons, so has three nights per week at home and four at the hostel. Laurence is in a double room at the hostel, the other boy being his classmate at school. Laurence's hostel is only for the deaf-blind children, and of the eight children in the unit, four live in Auckland with similar arrangements to Laurence, and the other four come from various parts of New Zealand and live in at the hostel all term and get six free air trips home each year (the three holiday breaks plus the Easter break and two mid-term breaks).

The Auckland children are allocated two weekends at the hostel per term in order to give the families an opportunity to have recreational time together without the handicapped child. This has been most successful and we all enjoy our free weekends, although there is no obligation to take them up if things are going particularly well at home at the time. In the hostel report of three months ago, the matron made the following comments:

Bathroom Routines:	With prompting can clean his teeth and wash his face. When having a bath, makes the attempt to wash himself but needs help to finish off.
Sleeping:	Goes to bed early most nights and sleeps right through. No trouble with wet beds.
Toileting:	Goes to the toilet without being asked.
Eating:	Eats most things but sometimes needs firm persuasion.
Medical:	Has the occasional cold and the odd ear infection.
General:	Is a loveable little boy. Plays well but sometimes needs a lot of attention.

Laurence is very happy with his life. He loves coming home but gets excited when I sign to him that the school bus has arrived for him. He gets a lot of variety and stimulation and a great deal of attention, and as can be seen, his accomplishments far exceed the gloomy pessimistic forecasts made for him by the "experts" so long ago.

Suggestions for Ways of Improving Services

Help for parents is needed even at the moment of informing them that their child has special problems. Doctors must use a sympathetic and sensitive approach instead of breezily making catastrophic announcements with total disregard to the feelings of the parents. This must be done in a manner which instantly assures parents that they are not going to be left alone to face the enormous task in front of them and that there are welfare organizations that can be of great benefit to parents as well as the child. There also needs to be early contact with another parent who has faced the same sort of problems, and who understand precisely what the newly shattered parents are feeling. Another helpful service at the outset would be to give parents a reference list of helpful books, or to lend them to parents if they have time at the hospital, so that parents can find out as much as possible about the condition of their child and what the future may possibly hold. When you are reeling from the shock that you have just been dealt, it is very difficult to absorb all the technical medical terminology and information that the doctor is telling you, and something to take away and study later would be most helpful. It is vital that doctors are well-informed on the functions of the various welfare organizations. We had no idea that Homai College, a school for the blind, had a deaf-blind unit, and we had not even heard the term "deaf-blind" and so did not know that Laurence fitted into a recognized category, although we had seen numerous doctors, specialists and were in touch with other welfare groups. Cooperation and coordination is required so that families get the best possible assistance.

The final point I would make is that doctors must not be so totally negative, but should say that there are some children who make remarkable progress and that it is well worth going to the effort of working hard with the child in the hope that it will help him to overcome his problems. The doctors who spoke to us about Laurence's condition and future could not see any bright spots on the horizon and painted a very black picture of the life ahead for Laurence, and not one mentioned any possibility of some form of education. The doctor must be realistic, of course, but I feel very strongly that parents need even a modest amount of hope and unlimited support and encouragement.

The next stage is getting to grips with the practical problems of suddenly finding yourself in charge of a child with problems of which you have had no training, knowledge, or experience. Advice and assistance from the relevant welfare services is crucial, and the welfare workers must visit the home regularly. I also believe that it is vital that the child be involved in an early intervention program right from infancy to catch the child early when the mind is malleable and learning can take place most easily. At a, say, weekly session in a clinic, parents can be trained and instructed in physiotherapy, stimulating the child in every way possible to aid intellectual development, etc., so that they can then carry-out home programs tailored to meet each child's individual needs. Meeting other parents is also most valuable, so that they can support and encourage each other, and the knowledge that you are doing something constructive to help your child is highly beneficial. This is also the time to begin signing as you talk to the child, so parents must learn to sign as well. Communication is vital but so often other avenues than speech are totally ignored until the child is at least school age and the important early opportunity is lost.

Once the child has been placed at a satisfactory educational facility life becomes much easier, but it is most important that the welfare services continue right throughout the handicapped person's life, with assistance in the areas of employment, accommodation, and recreation, so that the handicapped person may be as independent as possible and can lead an active and fulfilled life.

PSYCHOLOGICAL INTERPRETATION

Maryanne Ward

My first response to this story is anger and hostility towards the medical profession for what seems to be insensitive bungling. For example, to dismiss a rash in early pregnancy as a nervous reaction to being pregnant is inexcusable. In the United States, a malpractice lawsuit would be filed against such a negligent doctor. The mishandling continued throughout Laurence's early life: keeping parents waiting long hours, not noticing the cataracts early on, informing the mother "conversationally" three weeks later, presenting only the negative aspects of the situation, and being unaware of the community and educational services available.

It is obvious that one service sorely needed in this situation was case management: someone who saw the whole picture, knew about Laurence, and knew about resources available. As it happened, Laurence's parents were left to discover available resources on their own and it was only through a fortuitous circumstance that they found a school for Laurence. Before that, services were fragmented, uncoordinated, and sometimes inappropriate. For example, speech therapy for a two-year-old, deaf-blind child recovering from meningitis, must have been frustrating for therapist, parents, and child.

What a relief it must have been for Laurence's mother to find a school and know that there were other children like her son. What a pity it was that she was not told about the early intervention services so that a home program could have been implemented. The mother does not say so, but she must have seen the future change before her when she found the school program (and a label) for a child for whom she'd been led to believe there was no hope.

Laurence's mother was lucky enough to have a supportive husband and, almost as important, a supportive family. Someone did a survey and found that the support of in-laws (especially the mother's mother)

86

to be one of the most important aspects in a family coping with a handicapped child. She writes about the frustration at the having so little success, a feeling common in parents of handicapped children. Before Laurence's mother knew her baby had a problem, she must have felt inadequate when, despite all her efforts to comfort him, her baby "only wanted to scream and kick and fight." Later, Laurence's slow rate of learning and the unpredictable future contributed to the feelings of hopelessness.

Laurence's educational program seems to be a fairly standard one for a residential school. I am amazed that he actually uses expressive communication! It is essential that he continues to have opportunities to go into the community to see and (almost as important) to be seen. He should spend time with children his own age, not just younger children. A very important aspect of the schooling arrangement is that everyone is happy with it. The best school in the world would be inappropriate if the parents were dissatisfied or the child protested when it was time to go to school.

It is not too early to begin vocational training and to make plans for the future. Laurence's parents should consider what options will be available in the community for a deaf-blind adult and tailor all of his training and learning to prepare for those options. To accomplish this will require close coordination between parents, school, and community agencies (case management again).

From her written account, Laurence's mother seems like a practical down-to-earth person who has handled the situation well for everyone in the family. She didn't focus on any of the great psychological problems that we "experts" like to impose on parents. She does not deny any depth of feeling, but she emphasizes that her greatest problem was lack of sleep. Her suggestions for ways of improving services should be required reading for every student in medical school.

Mother's comments were written when the situation was fairly stable; a nine-year old who is in school after going through many periods of adjustment to reach this point. When Laurence reaches puberty, there will be another period of adjustment to be faced with physical changes and possible behavior problems. The family will face the fact that soon Laurence will be an adult making different demands on his parents and siblings. It will be difficult, but this family will succeed. These parents created a good life despite many obstacles in the past and will continue to succeed despite the obstacles to come.

LISA

Dear Fellow Parents:
I had this opportunity to attempt to put together some of the more crucial problems we have with our children's educational placements, etc. I have expressed to the best of my ability suggestions that may help cut through these problems. But by no means can I feel comfortable regarding parental involvement dealing with their deaf-blind, multihandicapped children.

As a parent I am very aware of the difficulties dealing with the bureaucracy, but parents have in many instances neglected their rights and responsibilities toward their own child and his/her future plans!

Please consider these personal suggestions—be honest with yourself and search your innermost feelings, and from there make any/all the necessary decisions/alternatives in behalf of your child and family:

Do you find it hard to talk about your child and his/her abilities? Contact your regional staff and/or state deaf-blind education consultant for assistance in reaching other parents in your area and make every effort to attend parent workshops and/or meetings in your community which will help you learn, understand, and accept the beauty in your child rather than only seeing his/her inabilities. Find ways to build a more positive attitude.

Do you know your child's teacher? Are you involved and aware of your child's daily classroom routine or are you afraid of educators/administrators? Make every effort to speak with your child's teacher, take occasional opportunities to go to school and observe your child's program and ask questions regarding what, why your child is doing specific things. Don't forget that you can be helpful by sharing how, when, and why your child does things and what and how he/she does things at home. Attempt to verbalize your feelings and possibly together those feelings fit into prospective—don't just accept everything the educators say or tell you about your child as a proven fact without discussing your opinions and ideas as well. You most definitely have some insight to share that may be more *helpful* to your child; don't allow yourself to be intimidated—you have important things to say too and you are with your child more time than the teachers!

Know your rights and responsibilities toward your child, but don't always have a chip on your shoulder when dealing with professionals. Join the ARC and parent groups in your area—they often can help/direct you.

Take every opportunity to attend meetings, evaluations, etc., that have to do with your child and could be supportive to you and your family as well.

Your child's IEP is important—learn to attend and participate in these meetings. The opportunities to share and learn is valuable.

Realize, we as parents have a unique understanding of our child that professionals don't have, just as they have things to share which would be helpful to us. Your opinion is just as important. Question them if you don't quite understand or if you disagree and then express your feelings as to why you feel that way. Remember no ONE person has all the answers. We must work as a team in our child's best interest.

If you can't understand the professional jargon or test interpretations, etc., ask questions; ask for them to use every day language. Don't be afraid that your questions will sound dumb or that they will think you are ignorant—without understanding you can't have input.

Make sure you feel comfortable with the goals suggested and ask for an explanation as to the bearing of those goals on your child's future; assist the professional in ways your child learns best, share helpful hints that may help them help your child better, and share your opinions and disagreements if you feel it is necessary.

Review your child's records at school periodically—making sure you understand and agree with everything within them and that everything is true. Make a habit of collecting and keeping copies of every and all evaluations dealing with your child.

If you disagree with evaluation results—know your rights—there is probably an advocacy group in your community; if not, there is one in your state education department. Remember, we as parents have the best chance of making changes for our child and others like them; do all you can to become and remain involved at any level. We could be our child's best advocate!

Learn how to appreciate your child and his/her progress, no

matter how small. Search deeply and realize each of our children is beautiful no matter how different he/she may be, no matter what they can or can't do, but especially look at your handicapped child as a loving part of you and your husband.

Realize the importance and learn how to be firm and consistent when dealing with your child's behavior problems. Work closely with school and how they suggest you deal with the behaviors—and develop a behavior management program that you both can use and feel comfortable with.

Don't leave out your other children or spouse when developing this behavior plan. Don't do everything *for* your child, but do them with him/her and try to get them to do things as independently as possible.

Most important—ENJOY your child for what he/she is!

We never really know how much inner strength we have, nor do we give appropriate recognition and/or credit; but I truly acknowledge that the Lord has given us that strength from the beginning—I just didn't realize it until I looked back to survey things and knew though we got through, and well at that, that we could never have done it on our own.

My strength then, and even stronger now, is only because the Lord has allowed me to see His loving beauty through Lisa and because of her has opened an entirely different, but fulfilling and beautiful life than I could have ever dreamed. God bless each of you.

Mother's Story

I could never have written this story of our daughter Lisa without first stating that by no means have my fourteen years of involvement in finding appropriate education/training for Lisa been negative. Through the many years I have met some very beautiful people—people I never would have met if it wasn't for my handicapped daughter. I have also witnessed that through my daughter, many of these same people have been priviledged to learn and experience many beautiful things. They too have grown emotionally, as I have. They have shared my daughter with her handicaps; they too see her beauty.

I would also like to say that by no means am I attempting to make it appear as if parents are all right and that educators/administrators are all wrong; on the contrary, I am very aware that we as parents have many faults. I merely want to bring things to light that I've come up against and as a parent feel that educators/administrators need to consider. It's so easy to judge, especially when you have never experienced a similar situation. I still find it extremely difficult to overcome the professional superiority and judgmental syndrome which somehow is so prevalent amongst a number of those who constantly touch our children/adults. I hope some of the things I have written about will be accepted in the spirit in which they have been expressed and that no deeper meanings will be placed upon them. Any professionals who know me and my deep love and admiration toward caring, dedicated workers in the field will appreciate why I've taken this opportunity to speak out.

Just as educators/administrators become frustrated, so too do parents. If my experiences both negative as well as positive help even one person it has been worthwhile and I thank God for the opportunity offered me.

Meet Lisa

It was April 1968, four days before Easter; I made my regular monthly visit to the gynecologist—"looks like *you may* be pregnant"; I decided *I was!* Shared it with everyone—why shouldn't I be elated? It was four years that Bert and I had been trying; I had surgery for severe endometriosis, then was on fertility pills for six months and finally for six months I'd received a monthly hormone injection, all to assist me in becoming pregnant. We were looking forward to this baby—any baby!

The Saturday before Easter, my nieces christening was lovely, but I really didn't appreciate it. I felt extremely achy, listless, and had a terrible runny nose—I felt lousy. I awakened Easter Sunday morning with a fine rash over my entire body and still felt rotten. Somehow I knew I had German measles! I panicked a mite—being a nurse and remembering what we learned during training (which really wasn't a great deal—not a great deal was known about rubella babies; not many had been diagnosed as such). My doctor wasn't upset because it still wasn't sure if I was actually pregnant...well, too late to worry now!

My nine months were uneventful—oh, periodically I was concerned about the "mental aspect" of the baby. No one really could tell me much and at least no one attempted to talk me into an abortion and I had no intentions of having one since it took us so long to finally have this one. All in all, Bert and I were excited and I prayed regularly that my baby not be so retarded that it couldn't enjoy life but more important that He give us the strength to accept what was ahead of us. Looking back, He sure has given us that strength. I believe what the Bible says, "I can do all things through Christ who strengtheth me"!

I was so interested in a baby to *love* that not too much else monopolized my thoughts. Oh being a nurse wasn't always useful—I worried most about labor and delivery—all the things that could go wrong and not all necessarily things that were merely due to rubella. I worked up until the day I delivered, which really helped me to keep my mind off many thoughts. How blessed we were to finally have that baby we had wanted and waited for all those years! And then the baby would move and reinforce all those positive feelings. This baby was created out of love and will be part of us both; I just couldn't wait to hold it and care for it and LOVE it. L O V E that was, is, and always will be the answer! The problem is in how we define, express, feel, share, and deeply understand the word LOVE. It's definitely not the mere selfish physical part but one's total desire to understand others, deep sharing and appreciating every and any little thing positive, total commitment in finding the *good* of each other!

December 30, 1968—labor and delivery were rather uneventful. At 1:50 P.M. a bouncing baby girl was born, weighing 5 lbs. 7 ozs. I knew that something was wrong; she was in the incubator too long and I couldn't nurse her as soon as I should have and no one could tell me anything— "everything's alright." Finally, the next morning the pediatrician (whom I chose because I'd worked with him at the hospital and he was the best) broke the news as easily as possible: Eyes: bilateral cataracts; Ears: questionable hearing problem; Heart: needs further evaluation, definitely enlarged; Neurologically: hyperactive, hypertonic. Nothing else could be determined until further studies were completed: She was in no acute distress and I could try to nurse her, but due to weakness she would probably have to be bottle fed. All my dreams of devoted motherhood down the drain? All I wanted was to hold my baby and I just knew I would be able to nurse her—so tiny. I'd never seen such a tiny baby. I couldn't stop the crying; she wasn't strong enough to suck well, but she was hungry. What an experience; the first time with my baby and I became weepy because I didn't know what to do—that too changed quickly. I had faith; I prayed and believed the Lord would help and soon I had special privileges and got Lisa *every time* she cried—approximately every two hours. She eventually began to nurse well and began to gain back those 5 oz. she lost after birth. Within 7 to 8 days we were discharged. We were bringing our baby home—how joyous. Bert and I really hadn't discussed things; neither of us wanted to worry each other. I think we felt like let's see what happens. I still think no one can or should attempt to tell new parents their child's ultimate potential when it's often based on books and their own personal feelings which are most definitely based on background and how they perceive what having an impaired child will do to their social status. Allow new parents to enjoy that baby as a baby and meet each medical-emotional need/problem as it comes. Most important, they're babies first—enjoy that—LOVE them for that. Their *basic* needs are the same as any other babies and love is the priority. I never felt guilty because Lisa was born as she was. I really didn't blame myself; my thoughts were already looking towards how I could make her happy and I knew we'd meet any/all her needs as they came—how else but with the Lord's help!!

June 1969: 5½ months old; right cataract aspiration. So tiny still, weight gain very scanty. Bert and I were quite nervous. Again, being a nurse gave me too little and too much knowledge, but Lisa sprang back beautifully and was home the next day.

November 1969: 11½ months old; left cataract aspirated—all the same feelings especially since her weight gain remained very scanty. Pulled through everything well as usual. Thank the Lord.

Between 15–18 months: weight gain very poor and Lisa began exhibiting symptoms indicating cardiac distress. Cardiac evaluation revealed coarctation of pulmonary artery—surgery not indicated now but possibly at later date—weight gain essential!

Lisa was rather a healthy child up to age 18 months, when she caught her first flu and was extremely ill. From then and until age 7½ years she had chronic ear infections (otitis medias) and fluid behind her ear drums, so multiple hospitalizations were necessary to put tubes in her ears and/or drain the fluid.

Overall, Lisa was a very happy, affectionate, hyperactive child. We struggled to familiarize her with night and day and the appropriate time and length of time to sleep. It was a long time job, but we finally succeeded after 8 to 9 years.

Overall developmental milestones were slightly delayed but not by much, and none of the major ones.

Since Lisa was our only child, we spent a great deal of time with her. I realized that much of the normal childhood development other parents often take for granted takes place because the children pick things up on their own through seeing and hearing; ours have to be taught these things and as Lisa got older we were still having to repetitiously train her on self-help (selfcare), and behavior skills.

Vocalization, visual curiosity, and attending skills fluctuated, improving for awhile then disappearing or decreasing for awhile.

Language, of course, was very impaired, but we never gave up. Lisa even started using approximately 15 to 25 single signs for several years, but not proficiently. She even put two and four signs together on several occasions, to express a thought during 7 to 9 years of age. It all looked encouraging to me, but the closer she got to adolescence the more she decreased the use of the signs; she resorted to occasional signs and gestures or merely did things for herself. This was where I had difficulty because our ultimate goal was independence, and yet in order to elicit language in kids like Lisa, some degree of independence is needed so situations could be set up to encourage language acquisition.

I learned as much as was known then regarding "trouble" areas with rubella children. Eating and chewing were my next area of concern. At school and home we worked over one year on chewing, with little progress. The problem was that Lisa became turned off to food, and any sign of meals brought about severe crying and refusal to open her mouth. I inquired from various professionals, physical therapists, educators in the field of multihandicapped/rubella, and speech therapists. No one knew how to overcome the clenched jaw. By this time we'd gotten her to at least eat a variety of foods and she tolerated foods that needed to be chewed, but cut into small pieces, so through it all we did progress even if we didn't accomplish the ultimate goal. We've attempted chewing several other times for short periods, but good old Lisa never forgot how to clench those jaws, so we remain today with her eating a good variety of food cut into small pieces.

Lisa was a very active child who enjoyed outside play—swinging especially, but playground activities and tumbling were a pleasure for her. To expend her hyperactivity and increase mobility and independence, we made our front yard a playground and it did all we hoped it would and pleased Lisa and us a great deal (by then we had two foster children as well and they enjoyed it also). Oh Lisa loved climbing, too, especially trees. Neighbors, friends, and relatives were awed and critical at times because we allowed and encouraged Lisa in climbing. They said, "She's blind; she'll fall." Only twice in years of climbing trees did we have to call the Rescue Squad because she just climbed too high and we were either too frightened to climb that high or could not reach her. But we all survived and it didn't discourage Lisa, so why should we stop her? She learned how far to climb and it never occurred again. As a matter of fact, we propped a ladder in the tree so she could get up and down more easily. Of course, I had to reassure Dad on several occasions of really how careful Lisa was when she climbed those branches to find her comfortable "perch." She always had to be bare-footed so as to use her feet and toes to feel and grasp the branches. She checked-out those branches for stability and firmness before releasing her hands to move on and she never fell!

She went through phases which were and weren't encouraging to us at the time, but I was consistent and had success in making and seeing changes. Bert loves Lisa very much, but has always left that firm, consistent disciplining to me and Lisa knew that and often took advantage of it whenever she had the opportunity. He never criticized or questioned my disciplinary actions and I'm sure it was because we both shared the eventual positive responses and knew it was all done in love. We are very proud of Lisa today and never fail to appreciate any and all new things she continues to bless us with.

Disciplining with love and consistency is a must, and though it kept me on my toes and busy on many occasions, then and even now at times, the end results was our reward and Lisa's too!

Lisa loved school and enjoyed specific adults—she was preferential and still is; you have to get to know her and she you.

Lisa's progress, plateaus, and sometimes regressions have helped strengthen us. Oh, several times we've been discouraged and frustrated, but we've grown through it all and realize that these changes haven't been any worse than life itself—ups and downs are a part of everyone's life, not merely families with handicapped children—nothing keeps you down long if you have a positive attitude and more important, faith.

I would say the worst and most difficult time through the years was when Lisa was around 10 to 11 years old, starting into adolescence. She had always been a loving, sweet dispositioned child, hyperactive, yes, but never mean or totally uncontrollable. But at that time she began some aggressive-like behaviors (pinching). Being hard-headed and determined that I would win, I just continued my firm, consistent disciplining. The behavior became worse and I feared the worse, of course, but again, through faith and prayer I continued the disciplining and finally there was noted improvement. Lisa was smart enough to know when and where she could use this behavior to get out of things (because we all know how most D/B go through times they would rather not be bothered and act like they can't do anything) and especially in her various classroom experiences where I have been appalled that behavior management is not understood or applied or just isn't bothered to be used. During these times, her pinching behavior increased and, of course, this turned off staff. Thus, often instead of applying appropriate intervention, Lisa was left alone and eventually she became worse because she knew she was being ignored and she didn't like that.

Of course, I'd be unfair to allow you to believe there weren't any classes where attempts were made to intervene in these behaviors. On the contrary, we had a great teacher who worked with multihandicapped-deaf students and who applied behavior management beautifully, and Lisa loved her and she Lisa. Lisa's behaviors improved during this time and she progressed well—then Lisa moved.

I've never hesitated to punish (spank) with love, consistency, and firmness and I truly believe that is the only reason Lisa pulled out of this terrible period in her life. In addition, I have always encouraged her teachers to develop and use a behavior management program in order to be more effective and not waste her precious time. We can't always use totally positive approaches—life just isn't all a positive experience and if a negative approach is applied with love, understanding, and/or appropriateness, I have found it works often faster and more effectively with our type children.

During the start of menarche, Lisa went through a great deal of difficulty medically as well as physically—a hysterectomy was done when she was 13 years old and a great deal of the monthly frustrations, impulsiveness with pinching and irritability has been curtained.

Educational Placements and Problems

From as early as Lisa's second month and even deeper now is my commitment to advocate for her and other multiply-impaired children/ adults alike. It is because of this total commitment and awareness and because I feel my ability to be rather realistic toward my own deaf-blind daughter and similar children and adults that I write.

I realized early that Lisa would need extra attention and that educational intervention must start as early as possible. With her severe visual and auditory deficits it was imperative to begin training immediately in order to optimize her learning.

I became immediately involved with finding out how deafness/ blindness affected the learning process, and had regular sessions with the speech pathologist, who was eager to help in any way possible.

It was around this time that deaf/blind children were being merged into the educational system. They were rather new to educators, so the old techniques that were used with either deaf or blind were being used. It was soon realized that those modes were not greatly beneficial to these children. This is where many educators became negative and felt the rubella syndrome impaired were profound and nontrainable. This group of children are profoundly involved, but by no means are they nontrainable! It has been over the past 5 to 6 years that through the efforts of truly dedicated educators and others in the various regional centers that more positive changes have been occurring for our special kids. Because of the direction of these regional centers, we as parents owe much gratitude and thanks.

In my investigation of public school programs at this time I was disappointed, finding that they were considering my daughter for a visually impaired class rather than a hearing impaired one—we definitely disagreed. It was very difficult to find classes for a young multi-handicapped child. I wrote to Tallahassee making a specific inquiry and found a nonprofit private school that would take her, tuition based on a sliding scale.

Lisa was 2½ years old when she started school and that is when I too became deeply involved as well, with the school, the teachers, and eventually decided to go back to college with hopes of gaining a degree in deaf education. I soon realized I just couldn't give up my life-long desire — nursing, which was my profession. So, I combined them in a way and directed my nursing to the field of the handicapped/retarded.

It was at this time that I also discovered our State Coordinator of Deaf/Blind Service and became very involved in attending as many workshops as possible.

Lisa remained in this private school until she was approximately seven years old. I was permitted and encouraged to be actively involved and the teachers and I learned as we went and Lisa made progress.

At age seven, I felt that she had reached her potential in the school, so I rechecked what was available through public school. I met someone who would listen and allowed Lisa the opportunity to be in a deaf class rather than a visually impaired class. I know without a doubt that if I hadn't been determined, and had valid reasons that Lisa would have been placed in the visually impaired class. Then and still now, our kids are accepted faster in a visually impaired class than in a deaf class, but I still feel strongly that deafness is the greater disability. I realize that the only reason Lisa was placed in the deaf class was because of my determination and because the teacher and administrator knew less than I did about rubella deaf-blind; they were thinking of the Helen Keller type and wouldn't believe me when I attempted to disclose other information regarding the difference. Because of their goals and illusions, they soon realized Lisa wasn't Helen Keller and the teacher often became frustrated and developed a very negative attitude toward rubella/MR children. Some of my personal goals and hopes had to be redirected, but I then, and still now, could not believe these children or any multiply-impaired child could be hopeless.

Through my many years of working closely with public school administrators and teachers, I have found very specific problems that I feel exist throughout the educational systems, but I must stress that by no means were all my dealings with teachers and administrators negative. There was a great deal of positive interaction as well.

Problems

Lack of Trained Staff

A knowledge of deafness/blindness is crucial to understand the educational needs and even more important, the effects of rubella on overall performance. Almost any type of a degree is accepted by public school administrations. Often teachers are certified but definitely not qualified and the system lacks adequate and appropriate inservicing. Those teachers who are honestly interested in attempting to work with our children and other children who are also multiply impaired have stated over and over that the schools *have not offered* them what they need.

Inappropriate Placement

In speaking with other interested parents, I found this to be a very crucial problem—our kids were often being "dumped" in various classrooms, but most often into what the system calls "Profoundly Mentally Handicapped Programs." These classes, in most cases, were staffed with certified teachers, but very few who understood our children's needs and often were unable to see each child as an individual with very specific needs and broad potential. The kids are often being molded to the classroom and that was determined by what other children were in the class group. These children too were often dumped. Each child's individual needs were not considered. I see nothing wrong with PMH classes if the staff are appropriately inserviced and some specific curriculum goal is adopted to meet specific child needs. The system, attempting to qualify for financial reimbursement, viewed the deaf/blind as all being extremely involved. They are, but there was little effort made by administrators to properly group the children, making it very difficult for the classroom staff to establish an organized, systematic program.

Lisa, like most rubella deaf/blind children, can easily qualify for a TMR class, but that is not the program she needs! If a parent has enough stamina to out wait, out wit, and/or fight (challenge) the system, it's possible to get something close to what the child needs. But fighting the bureaucracy is quite intimidating at times—many parents work and can't find enough time to adequately run the home let alone find time away from work and home for the multiple meetings, letter writing, phone calls, and other activities necessary to fight the system.

Administrative/Staff Attitude

I realize that educators/administrators have had many bad experiences with parents; their lack of participation, enthusiasm, and/or what appears to be lack of interest. They automatically assume that all parents are alike. Even when you're a parent with deep interest and concern and have investigated and studied, you are still often treated as if you know nothing. Administrators appear to feel that they know the child better and even when we as parents express our desire to participate and be included as much as possible, we are still excluded or overlooked! Often the professionals feel they know what is best and have all the *right* answers.

Labeling

I realize labeling to some degree is necessary, but often labels are too firmly used with little or no flexibility. Functional level should be emphasized much more than IQ and often is ignored. More often than not handicapped children don't fit exactly into any one range; consideration must be given to the *whole* child and not merely the results of a formal education.

Schools funding is based on labeling and, of course, the more involved the student, the more dollars are received. So, labeling determines the amount of monies obtained by each school district. It just so happens that D/B are funded under the category of severe and profound. I've been told that because of that, Lisa could only be in a profound class. Many parents wouldn't question that, but I knew that Lisa's needs would never be met in the classes available under PMH. So I had to fight to get someone to understand. Flexibility in education is often extremely difficult to find, especially for the more impaired/multiply-handicapped child.

Teacher Burnout

I've seen, over the past several years, a little change in direction of teaching/educating the more involved child, but still not enough. Teaching/education has been geared toward cognitive learning— this is what burnsout many teachers because they have been taught and feel kids who can't progress significantly in cognitive areas have no future potential or possibilities.

Teacher burnout is due to a variety of reasons, but one area I've noted is the teacher's inability to appreciate the "little" changes in our children. They depend on IQ test scores rather than functional potential, their comparison of our children to "normal" making them too critical. When they can't normalize, they themselves become frustrated and negative.

Exceptional teachers must become more sensitive and positive—everyone can learn something!

Our kids may never be independent but they can be trained to at least be somewhat semi-independent. They may not be able to work in the competitive world, but they can be trained to work in sheltered workshops and work activity centers. If training was more realistic and less idealistic, the student's progress (no matter how small) would reinforce the child as well as the teaching staff.

Poor documentation, which indicates, to me, lack of firm systematic teaching, creates an increase in behavior problems—which frustrates the teaching staff—BURNOUT!

Poor Program Monitoring

PL 94-142, with the mandating of IEP'S, was and is a terrific advancement in the education of the handicapped.

Student staffings, restaffings, and IEP meetings are being held to abide by the law, but goals are too broad. Because of this, precise needs are not being met in many instances. Public school administrators, when questioned during these meetings, claim that the specific breakdown of these goals (task analysis) will be done by the classroom teachers. But as mentioned earlier, few teachers document much, which is the only way to monitor progress on short-term objectives.

In some schools, the school administration will review weekly lesson plans, but IEP updating and overall IEP goals are usually not monitored. There is little, if any, required documentation to show justification for goals being repetitious, year after year, on the IEP's. With our type child it is quite probable that they will have to work on many goals pretty much all their life, but with the broadly worded goals and objectives and little or no systematic documentation to verify the steps within that objective that the child has successfully mastered, then the IEP, in my eyes, is not as functional a tool as it was meant to be.

Present Placement/Functioning

After a great deal of investigation and numerous discussions/debates with various Dade City administrators, the classes made available still were not able to meet Lisa's entire need.

After exhausting all possible opportunities for appropriate placements for Lisa in Dade City Public School, we decided to move to the St. Augustine area so Lisa could take advantage of the fine program available there.

Since we had no reason to consider residentializing Lisa, Bert and I finally realized it would be to Lisa's best interest to make the move, so we made arrangements that she be a day student at FDSB rather than a resident. On September 7, 1982, Lisa began.

The move itself was a great step in faith, but I knew for sure it was the right thing to do. Because of all my years of involvement in the D/B field, I was very aware of the excellence and appropriateness of the program and staff at FDSB and felt Lisa deserved that opportunity, especially since for the previous 6 to 7 years, though all her classes weren't totally inappropriate, they still were not fully meeting her *total* needs (developing her prevocational potentials and increasing her independence in self-care, adaptive skills, and allowing her to broaden her social skills). We felt that Lisa was in a crucial period in her life and that we had to give her the optimum opportunities, especially since the "future" was right around the corner.

She's adapted extremely well at FSDB and again truly enjoys school. She knows she is understood and appreciated for what she *can* do and most important she is challenged—at her level.

We are very proud of Lisa and we are determined to support her throughout her life. I attempt to work closely with the class and share my opinions and ideas.

Presently Lisa helps set the table with pride, serves herself at the table (not always neatly), is very interested in the kitchen, and often chooses her breakfast and lunch meals; she'll gather the necessary foods/supplies/utensils, etc., and makes her own chocolate milk if she decides she is thirsty. She independently goes into the bathroom, undresses, and places everything in its appropriate place, gets into the bathtub and regulates the bath water, but still needs supervision in washing herself well. She is becoming more thorough with brushing her teeth, enjoys prevocational skills/tasks, and is showing a good deal of progress and success in this area—even though she is not and never will be totally independent. There continues to be progress and by no means do we want a residential school to take all the pleasure, credit, enjoyment or blessings for this progress—that is why we intend to be a very active part of Lisa's life. We'll share her! With our involved home environment, I feel assured the chances for Lisa's future are much greater.

I have definite plans for Lisa's adult life. I feel working closely with the Association for Retarded Citizens (ARC) is extremely important. We have hopes of leaving our home, when we die, to the ARC with the stipulation that Lisa (and Amy, our permanent foster child) be a part of their familiar environment until the Lord calls them, too. In addition, I'm working with the ARC to assure that there is an appropriate community program for our children as well as other multihandicapped adults.

I have deep faith and believe that life is beautiful and full of love and understanding and I take pride in knowing we've had a big part in making and sharing this time and life with and for Lisa and other handicapped children/adults.

In 1978, I had the honor of presenting a Southeast Regional Parent Workshop at which time I took the opportunity to share my deepest feelings in hopes of touching other parents like myself. Everything I felt and presented then is still as meaningful and special to me today, so I would like to share them with you now.

I have heard often that, "Involved parents are more effective." The various stages we must go through to reach the point of effectiveness varies with each of us. For myself, after making it through the initial turmoil of having a multihandicapped child and facing each new problem as they were diagnosed and the multiple surgeries, I found myself in retrospect surveying the entire situation. I began making several priorities, realizing that my goals and philosophies of life were dependent upon my emotions, which in turn were dependent upon my mental outlook. I couldn't expect for my handicapped child what I wasn't able to seek for myself. I realized that only if I felt good about myself could I then feel good about my daughter. At this point, I realized that these emotions I had within myself were normal. Other parents were feeling them as well.

The realization of my feelings being normal and being able to admit what I was feeling made me begin to see my child in a different perspective. I began to find things a challenge and to use my concerns more constructively. I could now concentrate my emotional energies in more appropriate directions.

I realized by sharing with other parents that I was in return learning. I learned that we must not deny ourselves the therapy of weeping when things pile up inside, nor should we be ashamed if the time arises of admitting our inability to control our emotions and the need to seek necessary alternatives in order to remain healthy physically, as well as mentally, not merely for own sake, but for the sake of the entire family unit.

As individuals we all have needs and expectations in life. Sometimes we have to admit those expectations are not necessarily correct and, therefore, we cannot destroy ourselves with the futile attempt of forcing them on our children.

After surveying *my* life, I began to face the inevitable facts about my child and her handicaps and what my child, with her handicaps, had to look forward to in the future. In doing this, I realized it was going to be a long and difficult job preparing for that future, a future of continual changes on my part, continual emotional adjustments, and many difficult decisions. Now, with some priorities met, I felt I had succeeded a little. I felt I was being realistic, or as the professionals would say, "coping rather well."

I was now able to see more clearly what some of the more immediate needs were and how I could possibly meet them more adequately. During this coping stage, I feel my anxieties, which were often associated with my concern for what the future would truly hold, were now changing. I realized that no one could predict the future, nor would I want to know that far in advance. The future is and always remains a continual concern, and at different levels in life these concerns become more apparent. It is here I feel that we as parents play an important part, because it was here I feel I gained my strength. Being a part of what went on within my county, my state, and my region for the deaf-blind, attending conferences, workshops, parent training sessions, and hearing other parents of older as well as younger deaf-blind children discuss their problems helped me when I touched upon the same or similar experience with my child. So I wish to encourage you as parents to do the same. Become actively involved, attend conferences, absorb what you can, take it home with you and digest it for future use.

At this point I then discovered a feeling of purpose, and a more defined stage of commitment came over me. I felt I had reached a plateau where I had collected my energies and had begun creating more positive happenings. I was functioning with a purpose, channeling my emotions "positively" with an ultimate feeling of pride and an ongoing desire to help other multihandicapped children in whatever way possible. I was committing myself to learning and sharing with others like myself, attempting to educate those who didn't really know what having a multihandicapped/deaf-blind child meant, and especially, sharing my growth of acceptance, realisticness, and love with those parents and professionals still carrying negativistic futures.

Now I wish to share with you some very deep, personal, and special feelings and thoughts—thoughts that inspired me through my growth, feelings that make me proud to have a deaf-blind/multihandicapped child. I accept my deaf-blind/multihandicapped daughter for what she is. I build upon those small changes no matter how small. I make her progress or gains my strength, for every new accomplishment builds the possibility for further developments. This hope is my God-given gift. Without hope, where would we be? The secret, of course, is that hope must be realistic and we must not allow it to consume us.

Without my love through acceptance, without my support through encouragement, and without my guidance through discipline and reward, my deaf-blind child would not have made it to the point she has today. I soon realized that the *basic* needs of deaf-blind children are the same needs as normal children, different only in how I as a parent love my child and accept her disabilities. It doesn't matter what others think. Love isn't solely for the normal. The miracle of conception and birth is only known to God, and the birth of a handicapped child differs nonetheless as being miraculous. Maybe I can't understand why it happened. But to be honest, I realized how many other traumatic experiences had occurred and continue to occur in my life. They never stopped me from continuing to live, love, and accept each day as it comes; nor could I expect each day to be perfect or each day to be so easy that I never had to accept disappointment.

I saw that raising a normal child today also takes continuous disappointment, guidance, perseverance, support, and courage. Basing my acceptance on what others thought or what a person could or could not do or by their appearance was limiting my personal growth as a human being. I honestly feel that each of us has a plan or a reason on this earth, but more important, that each of us has a purpose. Maybe it is to bring us closer to love, to patience, to understanding, or to open our eyes—eyes that are basically self-centered or selfish, as is human nature.

I soon realized there was true beauty in raising my deaf-blind child. I thought of her as a gift rather than a burden. I felt she was given to me for a reason, not a punishment. I feel she has definitely made a much better person of me. I've grown in so many ways. I'm more compassionate, tolerant, understanding, and more appreciative of those little things. I've learned to stop and take a good look at life, survey things, rationalize, and make priorities in my life. I've developed humility, because through the years of becoming involved, I realized things could have been worse.

I strongly believe that each and every experience we encounter, whether good or bad, is meant to teach us something. Through these experiences we gain fresh insight about ourselves. To close our mind and heart is to reject possibilities of inner growth.

We must have a positive attitude and we must honestly believe beauty can be found. For every sorrow I believe there is a joy. It may be a precious smile or a giggle that erases the inevitable fact that our child may never walk, or it may be their first attempt to communicate with us—even if they are 10 years old. Those little things in life can have meaning and there are many of them around us. Don't take them for granted!

Allow me to quote something Dale Evans Rogers wrote (she too had a multihandicapped child): "Go share your comfort and your faith. As we use our own experiences of suffering constructively, we find our sorrows turning to blessings for ourselves and for others." I can personally say it has worked in my life. Try it. It can work for you as well.

PSYCHOLOGICAL INTERPRETATION

Robert Holzberg

The story of Lisa is really not about Lisa, but rather about the effect that a determined parent can have on the educational system. In Lisa's case, the services were in place to provide needed training, but those who administered and controlled those resources were not necessarily willing to go along with the provision of an educational package which the parent saw as essential to her daughter's development. Lisa's Mother found the solution in becoming involved in parental groups, in developing her own knowledge concerning her daughter's condition and needs, and in learning the law. While Lisa's mother does not state it in so many words, it becomes fairly clear upon reading her account that many principals must have thought of trying to lock their doors when they saw her coming. Her persistence in not only obtaining services, but in monitoring those services, certainly has made a profound difference in the educational progress and ultimate quality of life of her daughter.

Unfortunately, not every parent has the dedication and faith of this parent. Her dedication has been lifelong. Even though there have been times when she has been discouraged, as she freely admits, she has come back and continued the fight. Psychologically, this is a powerful woman. The condition of her daughter appears to have been the impetus for the development of this power. There may be some aspect of guilt in this dedication. This guilt might have been the result of her feelings that her daughter's condition is in some way her fault because of the rubella which occurred in early pregnancy. The power of the mother's drive however, is very narrowly focussed and does not appear to have been extended past the educational situation on the local and state level.

In reporting Lisa's home life, she relates a situation where she provided opportunities which might frighten the parents of "normal" children. Lisa's tree climbing and the provision of a ladder to help is one such instance. The danger is minimized in the account and its reported that "only twice in all those years did we have to call the Rescue Squad." Generally, parental overprotection is the rule when parents deal with a severely handicapped child. In this case, the parents avoided that trap. Again, the fact that overprotection and fixation on Lisa to the exclusion of everything else did not take place is illustrated by the report that two foster children were also included in the family.

The parents' religious faith clearly has played a large role in their acceptance of their daughters handicap. During the years reported, that faith has been unwavering and continual. Without that faith, the process would have been that much harder.

Generally then, when we look at Lisa's story, we look at the positive result that active parent involvment can make in the life of a child with severe handicaps. Hopefully, that lesson will be learned by other parents.

Section Two

STORIES WITHOUT INTERPRETATION

Up to this point you have read stories written by parents with psychological interpretations by authorities in the field. The next group of stories also written by parents is designed so that you can make the interpretation based upon what the parents have done and how the child has progressed. Do you believe the parents have taken the correct actions? Are there any steps which they should have taken which they did not take? How should they proceed from this point?

ANNE

Biographical

It never occurred to me that I would ever parent a handicapped child. Everyone in my family was fairly normal (?), and babies were always born with various degrees of pain and difficulty for the mother, but babies came out with all their faculties. Didn't they?

My aunt, viewing Ann in the nursery, said, "She doesn't open her eyes." I said calmly, "Little kittens don't, either, the first few days." That shows I knew about kittens, but not much about babies. My sole experience with babies was my first, John, and he was, as I was told before I understood the word, precocious. So I supposed he was normal. In any case, he was what is known as a "good child." If I warned him not to touch Daddy's desk, he didn't. I thought that was normal.

When the nurse, a friend of mine from high school days, relayed the doctor's message that an ophthalmologist was coming to the hospital that evening, and would I like him to look at Ann, I consented, knowing that, of course, he would find nothing wrong. However, he came to my room that evening, and pronounced her eyes unseeing "at this point." My husband Merle and I simply didn't believe it. We took her to Dr. X's (I can't remember his name) office when I got out of the hospital. He confirmed the diagnosis of blindness. We refused to believe him. Something, somewhere, could be done.

We took her home, I in tears, which persisted for days, until John, who was then three years old, wanted to know why I was crying. I resolved then not to shed any more tears. However, I had a feeling of a lump inside—where my heart was supposed to be—which stayed there for years. More of that later.

Meanwhile, my friend Carol said, "God must have chosen carefully for parents for Ann. You are both teachers and can help her." I never felt more inept.

My husband, his arms enfolding Ann and me, said, "Teach her to help

111

herself." He repeated it to me often. (Repetition is one of the keys of learning!)

Meanwhile, life went on. Ann progressed at the same rate as John had. I was glad to have had the "practice" with John. We didn't tell him that Ann had a handicap. But one day when he was going out to play, he came to me where I was holding Ann, and said, "Mom, when she is a little bigger, I will take her outside with me. I will take care of her." The tears almost spilled then.

We still believed that a corneal transplant, which was then a new technique, would solve everything. We began saving money so that would be possible. On a teacher's salary, it was a pathetic attempt. Merle's parents gave us $50 for a trip to Mayo's. We left John with my aunt. We stayed one night, saw doctors during the day, with a negative prognosis, paid our bill ($10) and came home and collected our children. I was determined, however, that she would eventually see, so I would have to help her learn how to live in a sighted world.

Meanwhile, Shirley. We hadn't planned on another baby. However, in the process of loving and comforting each other, we conceived a baby. It was a most fortunate "accident." She was a blessing from God, doing her part, too, to make Ann a "normal" person. Also, it prevented me from "spoiling" Ann.

When Ann sat up in her crib for the first time, I said, "Big girl." She garbled an answer. I put her hands on the posts of the crib and she grabbed them and pulled herself up. Again I said, "Big girl," and her face lighted up with pride and accomplishment. She learned to walk by ten months, always aiming for the light, either in the window, or from a lamp. She pulled over a floor lamp a couple of times until we placed it behind the davenport. Her first word was "light," and that was all she could see. When Merle came home, he would pick her up, and she loved to snuggle on his shoulder, and he talked to her. She put words together when she was a year old. "Daddy come home." Now, isn't that a sentence?

We were advised by another doctor to take her to the University of Chicago Eye Clinic. The result was the same as before. However, the head doctor said, "Don't do any more shopping around for a cure. Accept her as she is, but be sure to educate her. She is exceptionally bright." I didn't understand that a mind could be measured in a preschooler, but it was a comforting salve. Gradually I began to accept her blindness.

Once, when she was about four years old, she came in from play and said, "Mother, why didn't you tell me I was blind?" I said I hadn't thought it necessary. Then she said, "What is blind?"

She was fortunate to have an older brother and a younger sister. She went outside to play with either of them or both. The neighborhood children accepted her, and included her in their play. Of course, there were games she couldn't play, but somehow, it didn't seem to matter. John taught her to skip. She was delighted. She had enough vision to see the edge of the sidewalk, rimmed with grass, so she had a grand time skipping. Shirley helped her learn to roller skate. There were tumbles, of course, but nothing serious. If she wanted to run, one of the children would take her hand and off they would go.

She wanted to go to the store for me, as John did. And one day I let her go. This was the first of many trips she made by herself. I don't know how she managed, but she got there and back. I prayed a lot.

She went to kindergarten when she was five, at a neighborhood school that John attended. He escorted her the first few days, then she insisted she could go alone, and did. The teacher was exceptional, and Ann had a lovely year before she had to leave home for the state school for the blind at Jacksonville, 250 miles away. At that time it was our only recourse for her education.

It was heart rending to leave her. But the staff at the school consisted of exceptional people, and she was well-taught, and loved. On the way home from Jacksonville, after we left her, we were all feeling sad, when suddenly Shirley popped up in the back seat and said, "Guess who's going to school tomorrow? Me!" It made me realize that I may have given up one, but I had two other children.

Ann begged to be allowed to go to the public high school in Waukegan, where Merle was superintendent. He didn't want to take advantage of his position to ask for favors for his child, but Ann and I persisted, and finally he gave in. The search for textbooks was frustrating, but we were able to get some in Braille. The physics text, however, was an old edition—20 volumes—and could not be used. So I read her assignments to her. Those were the days of the reel tape recorder. We were fortunate to have one. Shirley was taking the same German course, so they could study together—which was good for Shirley, since she didn't like to study. And at graduation time, the honor student, the valedictorian, was our beloved Ann.

College, I said, sensibly, "You must choose a small college where you can have more attention. You will be lost in a big school." So she chose the University of Illinois. Again, it was heartrending to leave her there. But she made friends, found readers for all her classes, earned straight A's, and graduated Phi Beta Kappa in three years.

Back to the lump. In my chest. Remember? It stayed with me for about ten years. Then, as I was consulting the pastor about music—I directed the choir—he said casually, "You must tell me about your daughter." Then the tears came. And pastor and his wife cried with me. After the coffee, I revealed my fears for her future—who will take care of her when her father and I die?—What will she ever do?—How can she live in a sighted world?

He assured me that God is almighty and can order all things well. (Ann and I call that "God is pulling strings.") God will be with her always, he said, even when we are gone, as He has been with us for all our lives. We prayed together, and I left her entirely in God's hands.

It was lunch time for John and Shirley, and I hurried home, running part of the way. Arriving home, I was breathless, carefree, and happy. The load was lifted, the lump disappeared. I grabbed Shirley, swung her over my head, and set her down. "Mom, what happened to you?" John said. "I'm hungry." So while we ate peanut butter sandwiches, I thanked God over and over for His assurance.

Ann practiced baby-tending on her brother David, who was born when she was ten years old. She was home during the summers, and we enjoyed being together and having family outings; the Brookfield Zoo, where we told her about the animals as we saw them, and she ate popcorn; we had picnics with friends and relatives, all the ordinary things families do. We had vacations in Wisconsin where Merle could fish and relax. The children and I enjoyed the lake and walks in the woods listening to the birds, and the log cabin with beds in the loft, and doing the laundry in the lake using Ivory soap. It floats!

Ann had always talked of getting married and having babies. I let her talk, meanwhile telling myself that it probably wouldn't happen. But she and Dave fell in love, and he seemed to be considerate of her, and they were married. It was difficult again to "let her go," and I had to remind myself that God was watching over her still.

When their first baby was born, Merle and I visited them to greet our new grandson. Going home, Merle said, "How can she take care of a baby?" But I knew she could. She had helped care for David. The only complication was the cat, who was found a couple of times in the crib next to the baby. His sojourn with the family was terminated.

A few years and two babies later, she and Dave were divorced. Merle had died a few months before, and I was living in his hometown on Congerville, where my sister-in-law and brother-in-law and I had built homes on the old Kauffman place. So I invited Ann and her family to come live with me. I had been pretty depressed as a widow, and Ann was just the tonic I needed. We were both limited as to income, but we managed. I remember Ann mixing up a gallon of powdered milk every evening so that it would be cool—and palatable—in the morning. I was teaching in Peoria, 25 miles away, and Ann took care of the house and cooked the meals. Chris and Cathy were in school, and Micky was a tearful four-year-old. But with the love and attention from all of us—the preacher and his wife across the street and aunt and uncle next door—he adjusted.

Cathy and Chris practiced on their piano in the dining room, or on my piano, in the living room. Ann and I had some pretty good talks, and life was pleasant—and fun! Meanwhile, she was baking cookies and helping with meals for shut-ins, telephoning friends and shut-ins. She organized a young people's choir in the church across the street. I taped some of the music for her. She had a Sunday school class and I taped the material in the manual. We both sang in the choir and really enjoyed rehearsals. The director taped the rehearsals so she could learn the songs.

Meanwhile, Cupid (God pulling strings?) was at work for me. I had some business with a representative for an insurance company, who was a widower, and from the first date, we knew we belonged together. We were married and spent the working week in his home in Peoria, and came home to Ann and family in Congerville on weekends. She kept things going at home. She and Micky could go to the grocery and get what was needed, and we brought provisions from Peoria.

Meanwhile, Ann was dating a young man she had known before marrying Dave. When that broke up, she didn't pause to pity herself. She went to John and Marilyn's home in Carol Stream (near Chicago) and arranged for some training in computers, an apartment for herself and the children, and began a new life. Again, I had to "let her go." I knew she had a small income, and offered to help her, but she said she'd let me know when she needed assistance, and I had to tell myself that God was in Glen Ellyn, too. She finished her course and worried that she wouldn't be hired because of her handicap. She had met Pat by then, also blind, who was a computer programmer and he insisted that she *take* her application to Commonwealth Edison instead of mailing it. So she did, and was hired. At a larger salary than mine with a master's degree and 17 years of experience. She and Pat were married and bought a house.

Now they have a baby girl who is the joy of their lives. The older children are with them; Chris is in college in Chicago; Cathy and Micky in high school in Glen Ellyn.

She and I are still close. I write to her weekly, and she telephones me. We thank God for our fine husbands. We are both happy in our marriages and in our lives.

Parenting

When I finally had to admit that my baby was blind, I went to the library to find a "how-to" book to guide me to care for her. At that time, 1943, there was nothing. So, for me, the whole experience was pioneering. I had learned something about babies with my first-born, John, and that was to be a "guide."

"Remember, you do not have a blind child, you have a child who is blind." A counsellor said that to me at some point, and I thought about it a great deal.

I still thought that eventually she would be able to see, so I set about preparing her for living in a sighted world, which turned out to be exactly correct procedure. She learned how to live in a sighted world, but was never able to see more than light and color, if something was just inches from her eyes, but never anything distinctly—shapes, sizes, distances. (When Ann was about 25, she developed an infection in one eye, and it had to be removed. The glass eye improved her appearance.)

Back to parenting. Babies need gentle, loving care. Ann was especially susceptible to loud noises, and in her growing-up years, she could sense the controlled anger in my voice, and stopped in her tracks until the matter was clarified. A request was easily done, but an order was something else. She had to know why she had to do it.

Back to babies—Ann needed assurance that I was near; I talked and sang a whole lot. I put bells in my pockets so she could hear where I was. Brother John loved to hold her, and was ever so careful. She loved being on Merle's shoulder, held close, and being talked to. He said words to her from the very beginning, "Mama, Daddy, John, Ann," and many other useful words. As we put toys in her hands, we would say, "toy," or "dolly," or "book." She talked early, repeating what we said. I realized that she could not see my lips, so I spoke distinctly—we all did. She could not see us smile, but when we saw her smile, we would praise her, and rejoice. She can hear the smile in my voice.

That brings me to another point—praise. It is important to any child, but when a child cannot see what has been accomplished, he needs to be told. "Good girl," "big girl" brought smiles to her sweet face.

Feeding. This was not difficult. The doctor suggested that I not nurse her—he was probably thinking the trauma might "sour my milk"? So the bottle was easily used. When it was time for solid foods, I spooned it in. She rolled it around in her mouth, wonderingly, contemplating, and finally swallowed it and opened her mouth for more. No problem. However, when sister Shirley needed to be spoon-fed, and I, between two high chairs, fed them alternately, Ann took matters into her hands. She reached for the spoon—I had, of course, let her "see" the spoon, and groped for something. I put her left hand against the feeding dish and guided her right hand with the spoon into it. I was amazed at what an easy lesson that was! (She was hungry.) After that she fed herself.

Diapering was easy. She was unusually good—cooperating by lying still while it was being done. When potty-training seemed indicated, I put her hands on the little chair to show her the size and shape, then set her on it, holding her firmly. I said, "Potty." She repeated the word. We had success from then on. I set her on it at intervals, and she soon learned that "big girl, all dry" was something she wanted to hear.

Dressing was a companion to potty. In order to get on the potty properly prepared, she had to shove down the pants. After a few times, she was able to pull up the clothes herself when finished. She always wanted to do for herself. Merle's "teach her to help herself" was paying off. (I was told by some harrassed mothers that I was too lazy to help her! Maybe.)

Exploring is the characteristic of an inquiring mind. I knew that in order to learn about her environment, she had to explore. Inside I watched carefully, rarely cautioning her about things in her path. I thought she should find out for herself. She got a few bumps, nothing serious, and was surprisingly unperturbed about them. We learned to put the floor lamps behind furniture, after she pulled one over on her, shattering the bulb, the bowl, and my equilibrium. She saw the light, and was going toward it. (The first word she said was "light".) There were plants, for instance, within her reach, and though it's hard to believe, she would merely touch, explore the pot, the dirt, carefully following the plant with her hands, then go on to something else. If I said "No, Ann," she would stop, pause a moment, then go on to something else. It was so easy. Again, I would say, "Good girl." She loved to have John build a tower of blocks for her to knock down. They would both laugh, and she would say, "More." Later she would build the tower herself, knock it down, and laugh.

Being outside alone was a problem. She felt, I think, the vastness of outdoors. Though she loved it, she was fearful alone. One day we were in the yard. I needed to work in the house. I tied a thick rope to the tree we had been sitting against, with the other end around her waist. She walked with me to the end of the rope, fell down on her bottom, and laughed. I told her I was going in. She toddled back to the tree, patted it, walked away from it, sat down, and laughed. Watching from the window, I didn't get my work done, but she gradually learned to be outside and explore. John watched out for her when they were out together, and I kept close watch when he was not with her.

Toys. Our children's toys were carefully chosen, because we couldn't afford to make a mistake. They couldn't have rough edges, pieces that would come off, or metal that would scar the furniture—or the children. Ann's toys were chosen to use her sense of touch and hearing. We bought bells, all sizes, and strung them securely for her to shake, or pinned them to her clothes. (When she had children, she fastened bells on their shoe laces, so she could hear where they were.)

Soft toy animals were favorites and cloth dolls that she could take to bed with her. Sometimes there was hardly room for her little body among all the precious soft friends. Her clothes were chosen with texture in mind. Soft flannels, smooth, shiny rayons, soft cottons.

Mobility. When we were visiting, for instance, Ann could tell by my voice where I was, and wander the room, touching softly, unless cautioned not to, sometimes bumping into a piece of furniture, retreating, and toddling back to the sound of my voice. (I must have talked a lot.) I knew even then that I had to "let her go" and discover the world around her. And she wanted to be independent, to "do it myself."

A parent needs common sense, humor, tolerance, patience. A child, any child, needs demonstrative love, support, and praise. This will help him to be the best he can be, a vital, important part of the human race.

CARSTEN

Carsten was born on October 10, 1964 as our first child. At that time our knowledge of children was not at all comprehensive, but after a successful delivery we enjoyed great happiness.

When Carsten was 3 months old, we observed that one thing or another was not as it ought to be. Carsten did not make eye contact with us and he did not track things using his eyes. On advice from a public health nurse, Carsten was taken to a pediatrician who referred us to an ophthalmologist. It was then discovered the Carsten was born with cataracts. Several eye operations were performed resulting in some sight ability being saved. By using glasses (+ 18) Carsten manages to walk around inside without bumping into things.

When Carsten was 1½ years old an additional handicap was discovered. It was found that Carsten also suffered from reduced hearing ability and that in addition to glasses he also had to have a hearing aid.

It was difficult for us as parents to realize and accept that our child was visually handicapped. The fact that he also had reduced hearing changed our life completely. As one of the consequences, I gave up my job in order to stay at home taking care of Carsten.

Carsten's handicaps made him rather demanding of us. He refused to eat and he had severe sleeping problems, often he slept for only 4 hours a day. Consequently, Carsten took most of my time, and despite the fact that I did not have any job outside of our home, I often got too little sleep.

When Carsten was 3 years old we made contact with a kindergarten that accepted him for 3 hours a day. However, as time went by, problems also arose in the kindergarten. The kindergarten staff had difficulties in providing relevant programs and they found it impossible to take Carsten on tours, etc. together with the other children.

At that time we had joined an association for parents of blind children, through which we met a school teacher. He informed us that in Aalborg, a city 175 km from where we lived, deaf blind children were taught and

119

trained in a special school. We shortly made contact with the school and through several visits we saw how they applied special methods and programs. Quite soon we realized that this special school would be most beneficial for Carsten, who had reached the age of 5 years. However, we had to make a decision whether Carsten when entering the school should live 5 days a week in a school home close to the school allowing him to be at home on weekends only, or the whole family should move and live closer to the school making it possible for Carsten to attend the school and still live at home. We were not emotionally prepared to be separated from him and therefore we moved to Aalborg. Meanwhile, we had our second child, a lovely girl.

With Carsten attending a good school, having "only" his time off from school to take care of, and having a lovely girl to compensate for what Carsten was lacking (what a thought), we believed that most problems were solved. However, new problems turned up.

Because of our move to Aalborg, we had left family and friends. At our new location we had nobody to talk to and discuss our situation with. We had nobody to assist us when we needed relief, no grandmother nearby to assist when we needed an evening off attending a theater or a movie.

In order to be able to work with Carsten at home it was necessary as much as possible to be with Carsten in his class to become acquainted with the programs and methods used in the school. Additionally, it was necessary to take classes in sign language.

It was difficult to establish a family life in which the often contradictory needs of the handicapped and normal child could be fulfilled simultaneously. It was alright that the handicapped child required help with everything; it was certainly not alright when the normal child made a similar request.

Unintentionally, our patience was greatest toward our handicapped child, and at the same time our request to our normal child was for understanding and tolerance.

At the school, Carsten was intensively taught, but the results were rather poor. Understanding of signs or other forms of communication was hardly reached.

When Carsten was 14 years old, the first signs of puberty appeared, and at that time Carsten suffered his first epileptic attack. For a year or so, Carsten behaved almost like an autistic child. This was caused by the dosage of necessary medication, which made him apathetic, and was also related to Carsten entering puberty, which made him deeply engaged in his own body.

As parents to Carsten, we feel that Carstens' life has been up and down. Pubescence has been the most difficult period, not only because of many regressions, but also because of a behavior which in various ways was unacceptable. It was a period in which great efforts and patience were needed in order to teach Carsten how to obtain satisfaction within a generally acceptable framework.

On January 1, 1982, a new institution for deaf-blind youth (18–23 years) was opened at Aalborg. The institution offers living accommodations, teaching, and prevocational training. Since January 11, 1982, Carsten has lived in this institution. He is very happy there, and in a natural way he has made friends with other deaf-blind youth and with staff members.

As yet we do not know the possibilities for Carsten after his 23rd year, but without any doubt he will need care within a suitable institution. Our efforts in this respect are exerted through the Danish Deaf-Blind Association newly initiated by a group of parents of deaf-blind children in Denmark.

MARTHA

Martha was born on May 1, 1957, the tenth of eleven children. She was born being deaf-blind because of rubella. Martha's father died when she was three years old. Her mother stayed on the farm, which was remote and did the work with the help of the older children. She also had to look after her parents who lived in the same household. An eye-operation was performed which was unsuccessful and Martha had to stay in hospital for a short time. Because her mother was overloaded with work and it was not possible to take care of a deaf-blind child and there was no facility for such children, Martha spent her early childhood (6 years) in a day care center.

In 1963, for the first time in Switzerland, seven children, Martha among them, were examined clinically. In 1970, the first "school/home" for deaf-blind children was opened in Zurich.

In 1966, Martha went to Zetzwil, to the "Schurmatt" home, which is a home for mentally retarded children. She entered my class. Here she received her first specific encouragement in individual lessons. (Only in 1970 she could enter the newly opened "TANNE" school, home for deaf-blind children in Zurich where I was teacher and principal.)

I would like to introduce this deaf-blind child to you and to write a short report about her development in the 13 years that I taught her.

When I met Martha for the first time, she was a small child, nervous and aggressive. She could hardly sit still at table for two minutes. She did not care about toys. She touched things only superficially. The only thing she was interested in was her doll, which she dressed up nicely and put into the pram. Then, she pushed it before her, finding her way through the room or the schoolsquare without fearing any danger.

At the beginning, she was not looking for a relationship with children or grown-ups. When she hurt herself she rubbed the sore spot, never cried and pushed back any helping hand energetically. She did not have any means of communication and remained in her world of touching (near the body) looking for tactile satisfaction. As she was a lively child,

122

she did not simply doze along but moved aggressively until she was exhausted.

After three months, our contact started and with it her curiosity about the world around her. At last she developed confidence in the "strange" hand which guided her safely and she recognized the person with whom she had pleasant and interesting experiences.

The child who was born totally deaf-blind is not able to imitate the surrounding world and therefore cannot learn a language in the way the deaf or blind learn. Soon it was obvious that teaching Martha in a class was unsatisfactory. After my 9 weeks of training in paedagogy for the deaf-blind in Holland I was allowed to teach Martha individually. Only then was it possible to train Martha's remaining senses with specific exercises. Signs "drawn" into her palm and gestures were the means of understanding. With time she became less aggressive.

Very carefully Martha was introduced to the complexity of the surrounding world. Everything that Martha did was taught to her first thoroughly, from the simplest coordination of her body to the most differentiated fine motor skill.

The impressions of the senses which Martha had received without any order, at one time, became meaningful. She started to put them into an order and to understand them in meaningful combinations.

Soon Martha knew how to dress herself, to wash and take care of herself. Her skills have developed so far that she is able to make Christmas presents and gives them to her mother and friends.

Martha, 22 years old now, is good-looking, strong, and healthy. Her face shows optimism, although her eyes are closed mostly and "dead." She smiles naturally and makes other people happy, too. In listening to her different, inarticulated sounds, one can know her present mood. Martha had great difficulties in learning American hand-signs. Now, she knows over 60 signs and gestures.

Since 1975 (18 years), Martha has lived in the "Wohn- und Arbeitshein LARCHE" for deaf-blind young people, Ottenweg 20, Zurich. This small home is a "family" of 5 young deaf-blind and 7 caretakers (now 9 youngsters).

Their daily program consists mainly of practical work, helping in the household, simple work for industry in external "protected workshops," and the teaching of new methods in their own workshop. Swimming, gymnastics, and walks outdoors are other activities. Once a year, they all spend a week in a summer camp. Martha spends Sundays with her mother. A volunteer drives Martha home every Saturday and her brother brings her back to Zurich on Sunday evening. Martha's mother very rarely visits her daughter in the home, so I try to stay in very close contact with her and discuss all the things concerning Martha with her. The first two days of the week Martha lives with me and we have a good relationship. I am retired from the work in the school/home, and I am Martha's guardian now.

Sometimes Martha is invited by another family with two children (4 and 6 years old). This has been very successful as the two children love Martha's coming and Martha found new true friends in the children's parents and grandmother. The children also like the contact with the countryside where Martha's mother lives, when they visit her. All these good friends help to enlarge and enrich Martha's limited world.

In addition to this, Martha spends another three weeks, twice a year, in summer and autumn, in the mountains of Grisons. My holiday house is familiar to Martha and she thoroughly enjoys it being in a small company of three or four people. She goes shopping in the village and she helps in the small simple household which she can "touch." Especially fond of hiking, she walks up to three hours with her friends, arm in arm, through woods and meadows.

I should like to finish my report with this little detail:

A cheerful small boy rushes out of the kindergarten and meets Martha in the street. He looks at her pensively. Martha's friend explains to him: "She does not hear, nor see and she cannot talk." The boy replied: "If only she can live."

How does Martha live today? Some ideas.

Martha is small in growth. She does not show any sign of a development of puberty in her body (there is a medical answer for this), and there are no physical changes in this connection. Martha is clean and likes order; she also needs to maintain it to be able to find her way in her daily life (clothes, household things, working material). In this order she is happy and able to be relatively independent. Martha knows how to get along with others in a harmonious way as she has to live together with others. This is especially obvious when she spends 3 weeks close together with a small group of people in familiar surroundings on holiday. She loves to get new impressions and experiences, she shows a sense of humour, wants to communicate (gestures and signs) and passes her days in a cheerful mood.

Martha becomes insecure as soon as she cannot understand and touch the world around her with complete understanding, e.g., when she cannot put back things in their places. For her, that means that things are lost or they have disappeared. When she loses order, when too many people surround her, or when she does not find a friend whom she can trust and with whom she can get together often, then Martha gets self-willed and refuses to obey. Sometimes this feeling of being insecure brings back the old aggressions which she had many years ago.

In Switzerland we are confronted with the problem of deaf-blind *adults* now for the first time. There is only one "Arbeits- und Wohnheim" for 9 deaf-blind persons. It is under the same administration as the "school/home TANNE" in Zurich. This home will not be large enough in the future. Discussions about new living possibilities for deaf-blind adults have been held at various places, especially the "Schweizerische Eltern-vereinigung fur seh- und horgeschadigte Kinder" which feels responsible for this problem. There are some important needs which the parents have brought out:

a) small homes distributed by region
b) homes especially instituted and run for deaf-blind (by birth) adults
c) homes which are open throughout the year and which allow the deaf-blind to spend time outside the home at any time.

Postscript: There is a film about Martha (16 mm, 30 minutes). Title: Give and Take, Friendship with a Deaf-Blind Child.

JAMIE

The parent of a deaf-blind child must be mother/father, doctor, psychologist, teacher, lawyer, marriage counselor, sibling mediator, maid, cook, chauffer, representative, daughter/son, lobbyist, financial wizard, and angel.

How can a parent relate all the anguish, heartbreak, dread, fear, anticipation, surprise, relief, elation, joy, and happiness involved and included in living with a handicapped child. Life is filled with a sense of "unfinish" because you are always searching for one more thing to try to assist the child reach his or her *full potential.*

"Full Potential" . . . what a phrase! One easily filled with misleading opinions, because if you ask a parent what the child's full potential may be you will get a different viewpoint than if you ask an educator or a doctor what this child's full potential may be.

The first step for any parent in dealing with the deaf-blind child is overcoming the feelings of guilt or "why me." Next, a parent faces evaluation. This can be so ambiguous that you are never sure if you have an adequate evaluation. Evaluations should start immediately after the diagnosis of "deaf-blind." Doctors give the first evaluation and this evaluation follows the child and haunts the parents for the rest of their lives. The doctors first evaluation of Jamie was "put her into an institution and go on about your own life." The doctors reports are what educators base their evaluations on when they first interview parents for placement of deaf-blind children in an educational program. Most often these medical evaluations are very inaccurate and should therefore be dealt with as *one-opinion* evaluations. I cannot emphasize strongly enough the impact the doctors' attitudes and suggestions make on the parents.

First, educational and/or psychological evaluations should be done in the natural setting for the child. The childs' home with the parent, the psychologist, and any other necessary persons being present in a relaxed familiar atmosphere is one of the most appropriate locations for first evaluations. If this setting is not possible and the evaluations must be

126

done in a setting strange and bewildering to the child, the child should have at least time to relax and become acquainted with his or her surroundings and the people involved. Then there should be at least two separate evaluations done in this setting with same people and, if at all possible, a third evaluation done with another group of evaluators. Parents can give valuable information at evaluations since they live with the child. Granted, sometimes we are not formally educated, but *most* parents understand and can explain their child accurately.

After evaluation, any glasses, hearing aids, low vision aids, and/or braces should be tried. These items are expensive, but most parents will try to accommodate the cost even if sometimes the child does not seem to get any assistance from the aid.

The educational expense of a deaf-blind child is enormous! Some states have special education funds available. Some states try to utilize the "mainstreaming" idea in the public schools. Some states have crippled children services or rehabilitative services to help with the education of a deaf-blind child. However, most of these sources are not known by the parents and usually parents are not informed by those who do know because most people don't want to be bothered. They would rather a handicapped person be institutionalized and forgotten. Some of the funding sources in Mississippi are: Special Education, Mental Health Department, Federal Grants, Vocational Rehabilitation, Aid to Dependent Children, SSI, Social Security, Developmentally Disabled, Crippled Childrens Service, Easter Seals Organization, Heart Fund, Lions Clubs and other civic clubs, Systic Fibrosis Organizations, and numerous other agencies who do not openly advertise their services may assist.

Jamie and I were most aided by the "Mississippi Vocational Rehabilitation for the Blind." However, even help from a state agency has its pitfalls, or rules and regulations as they are known by the rehab counselors, and a parent must learn to assist these agencies in using all their resources to help. Most of the available funds are channeled into some educational program already in existence. I wonder, however, how much better educated Jamie would be if she had been taught and tutored by her own "Anne Sullivan" rather than having these funds spent in a formal classroom setting. Most teachers, I believe, would rather work using a one-on-one approach rather than struggle with the rules and regulations of the public school systems.

Jamie was born November 26, 1959, after a difficult pregnancy laced with anticipation. Jamie was born in eight months and after

27 hours of labor in spite of the doctors trying to stop the labor. She was a good baby and being young parents we did not notice anything unusual until she was approximately three months of age when we noticed that she did not seem to be bothered by noise, but rather would jump at the slightest touch or jostle. We then began to watch more closely and realized that she was not reaching for toys or objects although she would hold a toy when put into her hand. She barely blinked when we turned on a light close to her face. With all the fear and dread a person can imagine, we consulted doctors and were told that Jamie was totally deaf and blind. On receiving this news, I felt as if a ton of weight was being set on my shoulders. Twenty-three years later this weight is still there.

Our first battle with "professionals" started when doctors were unable to explain the reason for Jamie being deaf and blind. We were told that she was *congenitally handicapped* and no medical explanation was possible. This seemed hard to accept even in the 1960s. Even in today's revolutionary medical technology, after much searching from doctor to doctor and from every medical source open to a lay person, I am still told by doctors that there is no way to find out exactly what caused her to be deaf-blind.

If you are a nineteen-year-old parent, the idea of your child being handicapped, especially the firstborn, can either be devastating or challenging. I was saved from devastation by the challenge of dealing with the anguish of the grandparents. Her fraternal grandparents refused to believe that a handicapped baby should be required, or was able, to do all the "normal" things any other baby did. Life became a constant battleground with accusations from this part of the family stating that Jamie not be made to do such and such "since she's that way." Her maternal grandparents tried to cover their fear with encouragement and assistance. There were times during these last twenty-three years when, had it not been for my mother's encouragement and counsel, I would have given up.

Jamie's father chose to ignore her handicaps and treated her quite "normally" until time for school arrived. His reaction was "keep her at home, do not send her away to school." His attitude of wanting to keep her hidden at home and the accusation by his parents that I was putting Jamie into a residential program so I would not have to fool with her caused the first disagreement in our six years of marriage. This resulted several years and two sons later in a divorce. Today, I can say that one of the greatest successes of my life is the attitude of my two sons toward their deaf-blind sister. These two boys, ages 19 and 16, accept their sister as an ordinary sister with limitations. She is included in all their activities that she wants to be in. They never seem burdened with helping out transporting or other areas like cooking and babysitting. They have never been embarrassed or ashamed of their sister being different. They have always taken care of themselves and home while I attended workshops, school meetings, etc., in order to get further help for Jamie. In my opinion they are "fantastic." I, on the other hand, have tried not to leave all the babysitting for them to do.

The story of Jamie's education starts with John Tracy Correspondence Course in 1963, which revealed some of the possibilities available for the deaf-blind. In the spring of 1964, I heard of the Magnolia Speech School which was being established in Jackson, Mississippi, some hours drive from our hometown of Carthage, Mississippi. The Magnolia Speech School would not accept Jamie as a student because she was legally blind. This school's principal helped me find a speech therapist who tutored Jamie for one year.

Jamie learned to say all the letters of the alphabet together with several words and was beginning to say two-word phrases when her teacher informed me that Jamie just seemed to quit working on her speech. She was five years old at this time and I began to seek other educational sources in order to keep her at home as her father requested.

The next step in the educational process was an attempt at enrollment at the Mississippi School for the Deaf in Jackson. The principal refused enrollment because of Jamie's visual problems and the Mississippi School for the Blind in Jackson, would not accept Jamie as a student because she could not hear. The principal recommended the Helen Keller School, Talladega Institute for the Deaf, Talladega, Alabama, where he was personally acquainted with the principal. A contact was made by the principal to request admission for Jamie in the Helen Keller School, and he also did whatever was necessary for funding through Special Education. Jamie was accepted for a two-week trial at the Helen Keller School in September 1964, and remained a student there until June 1981.

Most probably the hardest thing I have ever done in my life is leave Jamie, at the age of five, standing at the door of the dormitory looking out the window as we drove away. Trusting strangers to take charge of your child's life is not an easy thing to handle.

I cannot relate much about the method of teaching deaf-blind children at this period in the history of deaf-blind education. Jamie learned rather quickly to do all the manual things within the classroom. She had already learned self-help skills at home, including bathing, dressing, combing her hair, brushing her teeth, putting on shoes, making her bed, washing dishes, toileting, feeding herself, etc. Our mode of communication was a series of our own motions similar to sign language. At the Helen Keller School, the teacher continued Jamie's speech lessons and did not use sign language with her for the first five years of school. At this time sign language was taught so that she might communicate with the other kids and teachers at the school. The record keeping during this time was very limited and there are no "evaluation reports" available to indicate how well she did on her speech. Jamie's teacher used a one-on-one approach and Jamie was progressing at a good rate.

In 1970, the federal government passed a law mandating "a free, appropriate education for all handicapped people using the least restrictive environment." This law became known as PL92-142 and established formal, structured classroom teaching for deaf-blind handicapped children. Many deaf-blind children began losing out on some of the finer "reading, 'riting, and 'rithmatic" skills but were given access to prevocational training such as typing, woodworking, sewing, crafts, etc. With formal classroom settings where teachers dealt with several deaf-blind children at one time, Jamie lost out on several aspects of learning, including speech lessons.

PL94-142 required an IEP (Individual Education Program) for every child in a program. This IEP was a farce as far as Jamie was concerned. It outlined all the necessary items in the necessary language for the school to comply with the law. Otherwise it was completely useless in Jamie's case and in the case of several other deaf-blind students I knew personally in the school program. The IEP was supposedly the parent's way of being assured of the most complete education possible, but how can you ensure that the school programs will give individual education to each child and not emphasize a formal classroom program that looks super on paper but may overlook the child's individual limitations and educational needs? No two deaf-blind children are alike and a standard model classroom curriculum cannot give the one-on-one teaching needed. PL94-142 was advertised by the federal government agencies as the parent's answer to educating handicapped children, but it seemed to be mostly a federal cop-out. If a parent used their supposedly legal rights to provide an adequate IEP for their child, they usually antagonized the school, which ostracized the child. I came to see the IEP as one of the most limiting requirements to come out of PL94-142.

My experience with Jamie's IEP was traumatic. In the school term 1978–1979, I asked for speech and communication skills to be emphasized in Jamie's curriculum. I was told by the principal and the speech therapist that Jamie had no background in speech and that she was too old to learn speech and that the teacher did not have time to spend trying to teach Jamie speech when there were other students who could benefit more from the teacher's time. I was told that the speech therapist was an "expert" in the field and therefore knew more about this than I did since I was only a parent. With much pleading and demanding, I finally received a tentative "I will try for three months" from the speech therapist. This was done with very little enthusiasm and for only a small amount of time each week. The results were not very encouraging and the teacher's reports left no way for me to convince the staff to continue speech therapy for Jamie at this program. Upon researching private speech lessons, I found the cost to be unrealistic. Jamie's lack of speech education is a result of inadequate reporting requirements, lack of adequate testing, negative reporting from the teacher, and nonsupport from the program as a whole.

Jamie has been evaluated for speech therapy at the Magnolia Speech School in Jackson and the principal will now tutor Jamie in speech, but the cost is not within my budget or means at this time. Hopefully, in the near future we can again begin to educate her in speech enough for her to have survival speech.

Much of the educational process for Jamie was trial and error on the part of the teachers and the school program. When the states required certification of teachers for the deaf-blind, the schools lost many of the good teachers familiar with deaf-blind kids and hired special education teachers who were inexperienced teachers, and uneducated in the field of deaf-blindness. This led to disagreements between the teachers and me in developing an IEP for Jamie for a couple of years and therefore Jamie lost valuable time while this was being resolved. The hardest thing for me to accept was the attitude of the staff of Jamie's school. I had worked with this staff and with the staff of the Southeast Regional Center for Deaf-Blind Adults and with the principal in developing policies and procedures for the school programs for several years prior to this confrontation about Jamie's IEP. I was completely unprepared for the staff's attitude of "you're only a parent and we are the *experts* in the field of deaf-blind." Since this field was very new to most of the staff at Jamie's school, I fail to understand how they could be expert. I was finally made to understand that they had had a "formal education" and that made them experts even though they had no actual hands-on experience with deaf-blind children.

The program at this time was in the process of modernizing and becoming a model program and had no time, or money, for an "individualized education program" for a deaf-blind child. This is one of the first ways school programs "handicap the handicapped." School principals are so busy fighting for funds, from any and every source, in order to develop model programs to impress funding agencies, education professionals, and medical professionals, that they lose sight of the original goal of individual educational programs for deaf-blind handicapped children. These goals are—and should always be—helping a deaf-blind child reach his or her full potential—full potential being an individual thing with each person and not the opinionated decision of a staff of the school program.

Most professionals in the field of deaf-blindness are interested in meeting the *legal requirements* first, the needs of the staff second, the needs of the evaluators third, and the needs of the child and parent last. This leads to unnecessary frustration on the part of parents who are already faced with heavy responsibilities of providing for a handicapped child. Parents need encouragement and consideration in their search for services for their deaf-blind child. Each parent is as unique as their deaf-blind child and professionals should not lump them all into one category. Most of our parents have *lots of smarts.*

During Jamie's school years, I begged for adequate positive reporting procedures. It is impossible at this point in Jamie's life to get a comprehensive evaluation of her functioning level. I can tell you from my personal observations what she can and cannot do at home. I can tell you from observation and talking with the personnel where Jamie is now working what she can and cannot do on the job. Vocational Rehabilitation for the Blind has a resume from the Helen Keller School which gives very little actual information as to Jamie's abilities. There have been few reports on Jamie's speech. Rehab for the Blind received a negative report on Jamie's key punch training during the summer. They report that Jamie's vision will limit her in any data processing field although she readily learned the mechanical concepts quickly. This report killed any chances for further training in data processing. It is imperative that reports and evaluations be as positive as possible in order for the individual to have future chances of training.

With inadequate negative reports and evaluations on Jamie it has been almost impossible to find employment using her full potential. At this time we are settling for employment as a sewing machine operator at the Mississippi Industries for the Blind in Jackson. Jamie lives at home with me and her two brothers and so far has only the R.E.A.C.H. program for social interaction. This program is sponsored by St. Richards Catholic Church. The Woodland Hill Baptist Church here has a minister and separate services for the deaf providing minor interaction with deaf people of all ages.

The State of Mississippi has done extensive studies and grant writing to fund group homes for high-functioning, deaf-blind, multihandicapped people. We have one group home, the Alpha Home in Hazelhurst, Mississippi, housing six males. These people work at Royal Maid Industries for the Blind. Mississippi has the Opportunities Unlimited Sheltered Workshop in Ellisville for middle to low functioning multihandicapped. We have a new program which is an offshoot of Royal Maid Industries being established in Tupelo, Mississippi and Mississippi Industries for the Blind in Jackson is beginning to work with the deaf-blind.

At one time, Mississippi had a Parent Organization functioning as a lobbying, counseling, educational, and representative group for the deaf-blind. We had an active Steering Committee made up of Vocational Rehab, Mental Health, Deaf-Blind, Employers, Social Workers, Educators, and Parents. None of these organizations are active at this time.

The majority of deaf-blind children in Mississippi seem to be in the middle to low functioning range and most of the funds and time have been directed to services for this population. Three or four high functioning, deaf-blind children are still struggling to get established in some adequate working and living arrangement. One is living in the group home setting and working at Royal Maid Industries. Two are living at home with families and working in state-supported industries. The other one is living semi-independently and working at Royal Maid Industries. They have only minimum social interaction with their peers.

Although Mississippi has done much to provide services to the deaf-blind multihandicapped individual, we have reached a leveling-off point. There is no growth in the area of service facilities for the young who needs companionship, living arrangements, jobs, insurance for medical care, and love. Any program I know of for deaf-blind over twenty-one is limited to eighteen months evaluation or training which still leaves many years ahead of the deaf-blind person and their families to try to provide adequate services.

With the economic situation in our nation today, will we continue to serve a deaf-blind population which resulted from the rubella epidemic of the 1960s or are we heading toward combining services for the multitudes of different handicapping conditions? I hope we will not have to lump everyone into one funding source or training program. There would certainly be no possibility of IEP's in a situation of this type.

I understand that the Helen Keller National Center for Deaf-Blind in New York has training facilities for high functioning individuals. I am not sure what the cost is. However, this program is for eighteen months only. Delgado Community College for the Deaf in New Orleans, Louisiana, has college level courses for the deaf and has recently received a federal grant to fund education of the deaf-multihandicapped. This program may open some further education fields for deaf people. Here again the cost is a major factor in Jamie's attending this program.

From time to time, I have been contacted about some person or agency providing a workshop to develop criteria for future services to young deaf-blind adults. However, nothing seems to come from these workshops except a raising of parental hopes.

Jamie's future will probably be at home with me. There do not seem to be any suitable alternatives available. Since we are a majority of one, it is unlikely that funds will be available for anything else. I suppose the ideal arrangement would be a group home with an attached sheltered workshop. This would give living facilities, employment, and social interaction with peers. Limitations would be the functional levels of the deaf-blind and the location. However, the future at this time seems to be only more of the same that we have now. I would like to find a tutor/companion for Jamie to live with. We do not have the funds to establish Jamie in her own apartment and hire someone to live in. Most of the housing funds available through HUD at this time are more attuned to the mentally impaired and Jamie would most probably become a caretaker in this situation. If we had someone with clout to adopt Jamie and promote her as Helen Keller was promoted by several well-known persons, Jamie would have a much better chance to reach her full potential.

No person, "normal" or handicapped, can reach their full potential without good medical attention, adequate evaluation, proper individual education, positive reports and/or a comprehensive resume, vocational training, gainful employment, comfortable living arrangements, love, and social interaction. In order to achieve full potential for our deaf-blind children, we must have educated, willing, doctors; open-minded educators; concerned governmental agencies; funding; and educated parents. Hopefully, someday all persons connected to deaf-blind services can join together and have one overall community rather than segmented programs.

MARCOS

Marcos (my son) was born on the 11th of May of 1972. It was 10:40 P.M. and the birth was normal.

Apart from a double deficiency when he was born (deaf-blind) he didn't have any other serious problems, only a slight heart murmer. Two electrocephalograms were taken and the result was positive. Marcos is a happy child always laughing and very intelligent. He likes to take sea baths and swim in pools. He learned how to swim by himself. He likes to hold onto our car and take long walks. He also likes to drink fruit juice.

My marriage was on the 20th of December of 1969 in the city of Belem, state of Para, my native city.

After I married, I went to live in Manaus, capitol of the state of Amazonas. I was still a student at the time, so I avoided pregnancy during the first year. After the first month of my pregnancy I got the measles. This passed unnoticed. I just thought it was a slight rash. When I did consult a doctor, it was too late. The doctors first reaction was to advise abortion. I was very sad about all this because it was my first child and also because I am totally against this procedure. When I returned to the doctor, he had changed his mind and said that I should go ahead and have the child. This made my husband and me very happy.

My pregnancy was normal and it was a period of great happiness for us. The day of Marcos' birth was the happiest in my life. After 15 days we noticed that Marcos' eyes were always tearing. We took him to a doctor, but his diagnosis was not entirely correct. We then took him to a second doctor and he stated that Marcos had cataracts. I took him to the ophthalmologist and this was even more alarming for us. Apart from cataracts the child also had microthalmic eyes.

Our marriage went a bit cold, but we tried to have fun and sort of forget the problems.

During Marcos' first year, we undertook three surgeries on his eyes, but none were successful. Marcos also had hearing problems.

At first he managed to pronounce the words—mama and papa. In his fourth year of life we realized how intensely he was deaf. When he was seven, he had a loss of 110 decibels. No hearing aid would be of any help.

As Marcos didn't retain his sight, we went back to Belem, where there was a school for the blind.

Marcos started attending the school, although the school authorities were aware of Marcos' double deficiency. The only real school in Brazil for deaf-blind is located in Sao Paulo, but we didn't know that at that time. We started to do our best to stimulate Marcos and teach him how to walk. The school was not equipped for these activities it just took care of the social and medical aspect of the problem. What we had to do now was wait for a professional (teacher) who was qualified to educate Marcos. With the help of the neurologist, physiotherapy was recommended and after a month Marcos could walk on his own. At the time we thought that the cause for this delay (in walking) was caused by our overprotection. We did not let Marcos crawl on the ground because he had had several infections.

Marcos was totally autistic. He ate well but did not know how to chew properly. He did not like to be pampered and preferred to be left alone. Up to when he was three he was a very calm child, but his inability to communicate made him angry and he began biting people. One day I was the victim and I slapped him. This was very effective. But to my disgust he began biting his arms and fingers. For five years he didn't bite anybody until recently when he bit his present teacher. That, I suppose, is because she was a total stranger to him at the time. It was at the age of three that he started to show some love for us. He would pass a long time holding a doll which he'd found when we moved.

When Marcos was four, he tripped and fell in the bathroom and broke his two front teeth. That might have been the cause for his delay in learning how to chew properly. We lived in Belem for two years and as the financial situation was not very good, my husband was offered a job in the state of Ceara and there we spent three very good years with the exception of Marco's situation. You see the state of Ceara had no schools for the deaf-blind. After Ceara, my husband was offered a job in the state of Bahia. We jumped at this because we thought that Bahia would have this kind of school. To my total dismay such a school did not exist in Bahia. Our last chance was, of course, Sao Paulo School in Sao Caetano do Sul. At the time, apart from the school problem, we had another big problem with a hearing aid company. They sold us a completely inadequate hearing aid which almost caused Marcos's eardrum to be broken.

At last we decided to move to Sao Paulo and start a new life for our child. At first it wasn't easy at all, but we managed to go ahead.

We also have a four-year-old girl. The difference in age is due to the fact that we had to take care of Marcos and this was top priority. At first I did not tell my husband about being pregnant again, but when I told him, at first he was a bit upset, but then it was alright. The birth of our girl helped us a lot, even with Marcos.

As I've said before, the only school for deaf-blind is located in Sao Paulo. And even here there is a lack of facilities, including trained professionals. The children remain in school for a relatively short period of time (4 hours) per day. There is lack of almost everything in this school, a room for physiotherapy, a heated swimming pool, and a very important item, school transport. In addition to that, the teachers are extremely disappointed with their meager salaries. Last year they threatened to resign enmass. The parents begged them to stay and they agreed. I'm just wondering how long this will last. How long can these people remain in the school for the deaf-blind in Brazil?

JORGEN

Jorgen was born the 5th of June, 1974, 13 weeks premature. His birthweight is not known. The delivery had been quite difficult and I thought I gave birth to a dead child. Afterwards, I was told that a nurse had heard a little sigh from him, and he was immediately brought to life with a respirator and put in an incubator. Two hours later, I was told that I had given birth to a boy and we had to find a name for him. It was uncertain how long he would live, but we christened him.

Well, Jorgen did live and he struggled for two months before he decided that he would live. They were two very hard months. My contribution was my milk. I sat pumping myself 5 to 6 times a day and had barely enough for him till he was 4 months old. He had many crises the first two months and the doctors just shook their heads, but they tried. We had 3 miscarriages before Jorgen and I was uncertain if I could ever go through another pregnancy. After two months, Jorgen gained weight very quickly and his breathing trouble stopped. The first time they put him on the scale he was 920 grams and he went further down to under 900 grams. After 3 months, however, we finally got him home. We were very happy; he looked so fine. But the doctors had warned us that there were some changes on his one eye. We did not know what it meant at the time, but after half a year we were told that he would be blind.

It was difficult to get information and help, but we contacted Norges Blinderforbund and got some literature about blind children. It was a beginning and when Jorgen was 9 months, we attended the first course for parents with blind children. That is, I attended the course alone because it was so difficult for my husband to take his vacation at that point. At the same time, we thought his hearing was bad. He did not react to sounds the way we felt he should and we saw a doctor. We were told that it was too early to tell, and since he was so premature it would take time before everything worked normally.

Jorgen reacted very badly to everything, but he was a very good eater and he was quite a happy child. I carried him most of the time when he was awake, and tried to stimulate him as much as I could. It was hard to tell about his reactions; they looked rather normal in many ways, but he could not sit when he was 9 months, and we were told to see a training institution for children with brain damage. Cerebral palsy was a possibility. Anyway, we got into contact with the institution and later he attended kindergarten at the same place. At the same time, we contacted the ear doctor again, and tried to test his hearing. They tried bells and other different things. Sometimes they thought he blinked at the right times, but sometimes there was no reaction. We tried a hearing aid when he was only a few months old, but we did not see any reaction, so we stopped using it.

After another year, Jorgen could sit, but he was 3 years old before he could walk. He did not respond to sounds at all, but the doctors could not find anything wrong medically so they assumed there must be brain damage.

When Jorgen was 2, he stopped sleeping during the day and did not sleep very much during the night. He made many sounds, but rather odd ones and he knocked the wall and bed a lot, especially during the night. It started to get on my nerves and I therefore managed to get him into a kindergarten at least once a week in the beginning. In the kindergarten, I sat with him a few hours then I took him home. He did not like to manipulate toys and he was not happy, but I needed some time off so I sent him in a taxi once a week for about half a year. During the time in kindergarten, he was not quite himself, but it was hard to tell. They carried him for awhile, sang for him, that was something he liked very much, then they put him into a bed and he slept, causing a lot of waking hours at night for us. At this time I got pregnant again and I had to stay in hospital for 3 months and quite a few months in bed at home. During this time I could not follow up with visits at the kindergarten nor the testing. We did not have any help at all during that time. My husband had to take time off from work and we had a little help from my in-laws for an hour a day. It was quite a time, but we managed and Vibeke was born the 3rd of October 1977. She was also 10 weeks premature. I spent another 3 months pumping milk, but now I could attend Jorgen and make up the time spent in the hospital. It took quite a few months before we got Vibeke home, and during this period, I visited Jorgen's kindergarten. Here nothing had happened, there was no special training, and he was very much alone. I was very unhappy, but what could be done? Jorgen screamed every morning when I put him into the taxi, but the teachers told me he looked quite happy with them, but later I found out he had never smiled there. The teachers were so surprised when he smiled. Something had to be done and we talked to the headmistress. She understood and we started to work more closely together. Jorgen started to respond very well to the music and to knocking and drum sounds. We tried to convince the doctors that he had a hearing problem, but they were not sure. A school for him with children working "normally" and only with hearing problems? "No," Jorgen had brain damage and therefore could not attend a school for such children, they said.

The years passed. Jorgen made some improvement physically, walking and running, walking stairs, and bathing. He loved swimming and especially running water. It became a problem because he got so angry every time he felt running water from a tub or the shower. He could stay there for hours and hours, using up all the hot water and never move.

We again attended a course for parents of blind children and again we were losers. The other children functioned quite normally and there I was with Jorgen. Unhappy in a new place, sleeping badly, not wanting to do anything, not touching toys, screaming when they played the piano; it was tough. One woman thought he reminded her of deaf-blind children. His behavior and hang-ups could possibly be because of his hearing problem.

We tried to test his hearing at the hospital in Oslo and he was given a shot to put him to sleep, but Jorgen was aware of something happening. He was very good with smells and he puzzled us at that hospital. We went into a room where the doctor gave him the shot. He said it usually was enough to make a child so young fall asleep. We then went into another room to wait for the shot to start to do its job. But Jorgen did not fall asleep, and after two hours, the doctors wanted to see him again and we were asked to go back to the same room where Jorgen had gotten the shot. To us, the hospital smell was the same in every room. As we carried Jorgen into this room again he started to scream and really gave us a battle. We gave up, the doctor followed us into another room and Jorgen calmed down and was alright. The woman who was with me from the course was very puzzled and told me that she now started to wonder if we did not underestimate Jorgen. We talked about different things that had happened with him that really puzzled us. He could do so many things, and most of his handicaps could refer to his blindness and his hearing problem. We were then told that the first course for parents with deaf-blind children would be held the same summer and we managed to enroll. It was so good for us to see other children with the same kind of handicaps as Jorgen had, and to our surprise we noticed that he was not so bad off at all, and definitely had possibilities if proper training could be provided.

We learned quite a lot at that course, and finally we understood his handicaps. We got hold of a book about deaf-blind children, and started to work with him. At the same time, we talked to the headmistress at Jorgen's kindergarten, and we managed to find a woman with an education in teaching deaf-blind children and blind children—not the combination. While we really needed someone trained in deaf-blindness, at least it was a beginning. Later that same fall, 1978, I managed to travel with both this woman and Jorgen's usual teacher to Andebu to see how they taught deaf-blind children there. At the time, this was the only institution where they taught deaf-blind children. I must not forget to state that the teacher for deaf children and deaf-blind children only, Anne Catherine, came to teach Jorgen once a week for a few hours. That was the only thing we managed to have the school board pay for. I will come back to that matter. Anyway, we learned a lot at Andebu and were full of spirit when we got home. Ann-Cat started to work with Jorgen together with his usual teacher. He was not alone with them but was together with 4 or 5 other very severely handicapped children. These were children who could not stay together with other children who were disturbed or could not function in a large group. Well, they started to work with Jorgen and it was quite a battle. I tried to use signs at home and gradually Anne-Cat, his other teacher, and I managed to teach him a few signs. Before Christmas, he understood quite a few, and the following spring he started to use some of them himself. Unfortunately, his teacher went on sick leave and Anne Cat moved out of town. Jorgen was getting quite good at the signs. At this time we took him for a new audiometric examination. I got really mad because the doctor continued to say that Jorgen's hearing was normal, and it could only harm him to start with a hearing aid. I told him I would take the responsibility and finally we got one. We tried to put it on him but he refused. He only took it off. They also told us that it was hard for him to have it on in the kindergarten because of central heating noise. We tried to put it on at home, but in the afternoons he was tired, so we only tried it once in a while just so he would not forget it. Maybe one day, we thought, he would wear it.

It was obvious to all now that Jorgen had possibilities. He still did not want to play with toys, but he was willing to play with us, fighting and throwing him around. His rhythm improved greatly and he could hum quite a few songs, that is, he could hum the songs in several song books and make knocking sounds. We could play quiz games such as "what song is this" then knock on the table and he would knock a few knocks himself, just so we could understand that he knew what song it was we were knocking. He was very good and hardly ever failed. It was the way to get to know him, for new people, and the way to calm him down. He could say a few words which were very hard to understand, but we could, and he could say "pappa." It was then obvious to all that communication was Jorgen's main handicap, blindness came next. To find a place for him was the main problem. The school board, the board at the kindergarten, and teachers from several possible schools attended a meeting together with us and the teachers who taught him at the kindergarten. Jorgen was now getting close to 6 years of age and he was supposed to change schools after he was 6. We talked and talked, but nothing was agreed on. Everybody understood that Jorgen had possibilities, but he needed so much instruction of various kinds that the experience was too high. A solution was not found and Jorgen continued for another year as before. His permanent teacher was on sick leave and only temporaries worked with him. It was a very hard time both for him and for us. But what could we do? Nothing was done by either the school board or the institution he attended. It was quite obvious to all that Jorgen was unhappy. Nothing new was happening to him. They still used the same signs he had learned the year before, and some substitute teachers did not use them at all. I tried to visit the kindergarten once a month, but in-between my visits they did not use signs, and I was told I upset the other children by coming so often. I finally got mad. We did not know how long his regular teacher would stay on sick leave. The temporaries were nice, but we were not getting anywhere. I called the school board again, the doctors, inspectors, and every other person I could think of who might help. The headmistress at the kindergarten was a great help and she pushed where she could. I cried on the phone, yelled, and was rather rude. I told them I would not tolerate losing another year.

New meetings were held and finally we managed to have the otologist at the meeting. He reported that medically Jorgen did not have a hearing problem, but agreed that he should be given a chance at the school for deaf children if the headmaster for that school agreed. The headmaster was a man of action. He found a girl willing to start Jorgen's education and after Jorgen turned 7 he started at the school for deaf children. That same summer we also managed to get a hearing aid on, and Jorgen seemed happy with it.

During the following year, Jorgen changed and improved enormously. First, we used signs and gradually language. Jorgen learned very quickly. After we got another hearing aid, now one for each ear, it was wonderful. Jorgen learned new words everyday, and soon whole sentences. He has changed tremendously. He likes many things and he takes the initiative. He has a good sense of humor and has started to tease us. Things that are not allowed he does with a big grin on his face. His emotions are more and more normal and his whole face is coming to life. Nobody can see now on his face that he is handicapped. It's like a fairytale to us. The people working with him are full of hope. This fall, his teacher will start with the alphabet and she is quite sure he will learn quickly. He can wait now and we can tell him what will happen next, and the next day even take a few days in advance telling him his schedule. At night he must always be told what is going to happen tomorrow, from eating breakfast to driving to school, what will happen at school, and so on. Of course, he still has his hang-ups. New stairs are hard to pass without walking up and down many times. He still does not want to play with toys. Running water can also be a problem, but he is slowly getting over that. We have managed to get him out of diapers both night and day—daytime almost two years ago, but just recently nightly. It was a big day. He's telling us now when he wants to go to the bathroom, but we still have a problem in having him go on his own. He must always have a person with him. We cannot expect wonders overnight, but now he is a joy.

Problems Created Within the Family

Of course, we have had many crises within the family. The initial shock of having a handicapped child was great. It required too much physical work. I got tired and never thought of myself. The children took all my time. Our hopes for our children, all our expectations for the new child, a very much wanted child after 3 miscarriages were smashed. We were uncertain if we could manage and cope with all the problems and worries. We never got enough sleep during the night. The sting inside our hearts, our tears, our hopelessness, it was a very difficult time. We argued and quarelled, but all things considered, we grew quite a bit through the challenge. We had to change our daily lives. My husband had to help quite a lot; his job had to suffer a bit. He had to take off many extra days to help me. He had no family to help us, so we had to work our way through all the problems ourselves. We feel at times that we neglected our other child. Jorgen takes most of our time when he is at home, and we always have to help him with clothes, stimulating him, and singing, so our little girl has to wait. She is not the type to wait and she very early had to help herself. In the afternoons, Torgeir always takes Jorgen for a walk and Vibeke feels that he takes Jorgen all the time and she gets angry. Our own hobbies had to be put aside and we feel sometimes the need to be alone, doing something we would like to do. Holidays are often a problem. I can manage both children for a while a few hours before dinner, but for a whole day it is very hard. Both children are home at the same time and I really get exhausted and look forward to my husband taking over. I am often tired, have depressed periods, and take out my anger on my husband. I feel sometimes fed-up with everything. I would like to get out and have a job and do something else and we argue, but we usually manage to get over it and mostly we have a good marriage. We have passed the bad things and now since Jorgen is doing better, we have managed to find a woman who takes him 10 hours a week. She also helps me the days he is out of school. It gives me time to take care of my daughter and twice a week daddy is only Vibeke's. This summer we also managed to get him into a summer camp for 14 days and we have had a summer trainee, a girl helping us with Jorgen for 14 days, paid for by the Cerebral Palsy Association.

As you have seen, we have had great problems finding educational placement. In Norway, there has been no training for teachers of the deaf-blind. Just recently a school has started for training teachers of the multihandicapped. Six have finished, all staying in Oslo. Until now the teachers we have had in Norway have learned by experience and by attending courses abroad. In Bergen, there are still no other children diagnosed as deaf-blind, or they may be misplaced. It is understandable that there are no existing schools, but the hardships for us as parents in our efforts to be heard is immense. To get Jurgen into the school where we wanted him to go was made almost impossible by the doctor because of his misdiagnosis of brain damage. Additionally, we could never get more hours from Anne-Cat. The 5 hours she spent were split between a few other children at the institution. To get those few hours, I had to talk to the personnel manager for all schools in Bergen. Later, to find a suitable placement when Jorgen was 5 was almost impossible. Nobody wanted to have him; he needed so many things including such special-ized personnel. Even now the teacher is not Jorgen's for the whole time—only three-quarters time. I still think he has too few hours. His placement in this school is not permanent either. It is actually a school for young children, from 5 to 7 years of age. Soon he will be too big and the future is still uncertain. We can only take one year at a time. But now, thank God, the experts can see that it was the right placement and Jergen has developed much more than anyone expected, and that means a lot. We are full of hopes for the future and hope that Jorgen will be able to stay at home. Later, it will not be so hard to send him away to attend school. So, the hardship is over, at least as far as finding a proper educational setting is concerned.

We really thought this summer would expend our last resources, being alone with Jorgen and Vibeke for 2 whole months, but it all turned out so well. We are riding on a wave top now. All of Jorgen's hang-ups were difficult, but it all boiled down to lack of communication. Our main problem then was language. It was a great day when he started to understand words, specifically one word "afterwards." Something happened to Jorgen when he understood that word. "First eat your things or whatever, *AFTERWARDS* we can do this or that.

We tested Jorgen's hearing again under full narcosis. The test was quite uncertain, because he certainly hears more than the test shows. He can hear a little up to a certain level. Jorgen hears music high and low, so one doctor said it was quite uncertain what route the hearing takes. The doctors do not agree, but at least we now have it on paper that Jorgen belongs in the school where he now has classes. Another thing that occurred is that Jorgen learned the TADOMA method his own way. Before we started with his hearing aid, Jorgen always wanted to hold his hand on our throats and then on our mouths. We never thought much of it. He seemed to get a lot of words in that way—long before he could speak himself. He was mostly interested in singing and that's why he learned the words. When they came out again they sounded strange, but we could understand what he was singing because of the tune. Later we saw a TV program about an American who used the TADOMA system. He was very good at speechreading. He could even "hear" music played by certain instruments. Then we said, "Boy, that's just what Jorgen has been doing." So now he continues to hold his hand to our lips to get a better understanding of what we are saying. He also puts his hand to our lips if he does not wear his hearing aid. He is really quite good at understanding what we are saying. Another thing we have noticed is that his hearing is either getting better or he is concentrating more on the sounds. He picks up language from quite a distance now, and he can even hear a little better without his aid. We put in the aid early in the morning and he wears it till bedtime. If something goes wrong with the aid, he tells us that "Jorgen has aid on," and usually something is wrong with it.

We are quite satisfied with the present situation. Jorgen needs more hours of training because it is difficult to work on new things at home. We would also like someone to come to our house to teach us too, but in all we are very well off. Jorgen is functioning beyond expectations and the experts agree. The big question is where he will continue his schooling. It is possible that as Jorgen progresses, his handicap will change from being deaf-blind to blindness only. If that happens, his school and teacher will change altogether. But that is for the future to tell.

This all we have. I'm sure we have forgotten many things. It is not easy to write this story. We have done our best and we hope it will contribute a bit and shed a little light on our life. It is hard to remember the past. The good things we remember, but the bad things we forget, thank goodness.

We are looking forward to Jorgen's progress. We have put the bad things behind us and now we are only looking forward.

THE CASE OF "C"

C. is a single child, born on November 28, 1963, after a normal pregnancy. She looked normal except for bilateral eye problems. Her very weak visual faculty disappeared after a few years. The first operation was performed when C. was just 11 days old. Ten other operations were performed during the next two years. As a result of these repeated and long stays in the hospital, C. developed autistic-like behaviors. She rejected everything, refused to eat with a spoon, and started walking only when she was four years old. C. had a very good relationship with her father and enjoyed his jokes; on the other hand, it was very difficult for mother to develop an attachment: she had to take the child in hospital again and again; she had to torture the child cleaning her eyes everyday. C. disliked women on the whole; in fact, they played a very negative role in her life (nurses!). When C. was two years old, we learned through a newspaper article that a blind woman planned to organize a kindergarten for blind children in our town. We came into contact with this woman and C. was accepted to go there. (At that time, we were still of the opinion that C. was only blind.) C. stayed there until she was eight. When she was five, we recognized that obviously something was wrong with her hearing. Though she made use of her voice, she didn't develop any language. A hearing training was carried out on a regular basis to eliminate locomotion troubles; C. got physiotherapy twice a week. This therapy was successful and was stopped when C. was 8. At that time, she had to leave the kindergarten. To our sorrow, she went to a school for deaf-blind children in Fribourg. Just at that point, she was becoming confident and interested in her environment, and we were afraid that this separation could cause a relapse into autism. On the other hand, we were grateful that C. was getting an adequate education.

At the beginning, C.'s development was satisfactory, and the relationship with her governess was good as well. C. came home every weekend and enjoyed this very much, but she was very sad each time she had to go back to school. Unfortunately, C. gets a different governess every year;

148

these changes always caused a severe shock and relapse. At the end of 1976, C. lost the governess she had developed the strongest affection for. The result was dramatic: C. started tearing out her hair, biting and hitting herself. The consequences were a mutilated ear, a crushed eye, and arms full of scars. In that condition, she was, of course, hardly ready for any work, just the opposite. At home, she distressed her mother and seemed to get pleasure from driving her mad. Of course, C. was in the midst of puberty. When she was 17, her behavior turned better, she became more open, and started developing communication (hand alphabet and gestures). Obviously she had made progress, but she was still not ready to make use of her knowledge. The same as before, C. is very unhappy when she has to go back to school.

Nevertheless, the headmistress is convinced that C. can make progress, so she is allowed to go to school for two years more. C. is now 19 years old, completely blind, cannot speak nor hear and is not yet "clean." She is able to dress and undress herself, but she needs supervising for everything she does. She has a cheerful character, a good sense of humour and a pronounced self-will. The future is still somewhat uncertain; in Switzerland, there is just one organization taking care of grown-up (by birth) deaf-blind persons, and till now, C. is not up to the standards set there.

A final remark: It was not so difficult for us to accept the handicap of our child, but it was (and it is) very difficult to stand the world around us.

STORY WRITTEN BY A
HANDICAPPED CHILD NOW GROWN

ANNA

Before I started high school, the guidance counselor said, "what do you plan to do when you grow up?" "My parents are both teachers" I answered, "and I will probably be one too." His voice became stern. "Lets face it, Anna, you are blind!" Paul, a graduate student was writing a paper. "How do you think blindness will affect your employability?" he asked. "I suppose it has to be a factor," I said, "but if I am good enough, it shouldn't matter all that much." The following year, a grad student myself, I found Paul's notes. He had interviewed every blind student on campus and without exception, without experience, we had made similar responses to his questions. There was a file card for each of us, the last one bearing a single line of braille. "Paul, it's shit to be blind." Because I had never looked at it that way, because that was in a world before I had children or wrote computer programs that blew up, the use of the strong language startled me profoundly. The thought, the idea was new. I considered deeply for six weeks what Paul in his supposed privacy had written, at length decided that he was right.

In his book, *Blindness, What Is It, How To Live With It,* Father Richard Carroll defines the greatest areas of lack for a newly blinded individual as (1) communication and (2) mobility, and he is correct. I think it's valid to say that for a congenitally-blinded person this is also true, communication with oneself (am I attractive?), with one's peers (do I really belong), and with the environment (is there a curb?, am I in the middle of the street?).

Communication with oneself. Most blind people are fat (when are you really fat?) They talk too loud because they can't see the person they are talking to, and they can't tell if he is hearing them. Their facial expressions are at best noncommunicative and sometimes downright misleading. (My daughter sometimes asks why I look so sad.) Even though they usually speak clearly, blind people don't move their mouths a lot when

150

they talk. It is almost impossible for a deaf person to lipread a blind person. Fingernails, if they are long, get in the way when I type, play the piano, clean out the drain in the sink. Why can't I just bite them nice and short (God made teeth before men invented scissors). Hair, clean and brushed ought to be enough. Clothes, why are things stylish only if they are tight? What is too tight? What is too long? If I finally learn to make these judgments, will they be valid next year, next week, tomorrow? How can I pretend to be the equal of my sighted fellows when 80 percent of learning is visual? How can I value myself knowing that I am not equal. Can they value me? With others, the idea that I was to look at the eyes of someone speaking with me was at first bizarre, and I still forget to do it much of the time. It seems natural to me to direct my eyes toward the place where the sound is coming from, the mouth rather than some indefinite place above the sound. Talking and walking are particularly difficult as my feet tend to go in the direction I am facing and I am apt to step on the person I am talking to. With others, a blind kid doesn't know that he must not (in public) pick his nose, bite his hangnails till they bleed (he may never learn that), scratch himself or even touch some places, or inform himself about other people/things by touching or sniffing them. If the parents' intent is that their child should live a normal life, it is absolutely imperative that they define for him which actions are and which are not socially correct, and that they consistantly evaluate his behavior for him. If the child ever hopes to be "one of the guys," he absolutely must learn how important it is for him to appear as much like them as he possibly can. With his environment, the world is made of, by and for people who can see. A few examples. Shopping. Both department and grocery stores. A blind person cannot select a peach, find the notebook paper. He cannot window shop unless by phone (for windows). A kid cannot buy pop or candy, and a teen can just forget about sneaking cigarettes or beer. He can't operate a candybar machine or be independent through the line at the cafeteria or graciously pour a friend a glass of water (where have those fingers been?). Eating is difficult, keeping food from sliding off the edge of the plate or off the fork. If I didn't enjoy it so much I would forgo the hassle altogether. It is impossible to always get a reasonable sized bite of ice cream on a spoon or to cut a steak. You eat the fat because it is easier than sorting or spitting it out. Using unfamiliar flatware is even a hassle because you judge the size of the bite by the weight of the utensil, and a sterling silver fork empty weighs as much as a stainless steel utensil full. I don't eat salad in public or butter bread or eat tacos if I can avoid it. I never request a fruit plate on a bed of lettuce. Often, especially when Pat, my husband, and I go out for dinner, I ask the waitress to have the meat cut in the kitchen before it is served. Other wonderful things that are hard to eat include baked potatoes, broccoli, pie, watermelon, fried chicken, fresh strawberries, (big ones roll right onto your lap), anything you are supposed to fork but really ought to pick up (burritos) or glue together (peas). Finding things when you drop them is difficult. Often they scoot; sometimes they roll. I lay my cane flat on the floor and make a circle with it to search for things. Sometimes I even find them. At work, people pick them up for me. Although meant kindly, this makes me appear incompetent. Finding things when you put them somewhere. A place for everything and everything in its place was never more relevant. Sighted people forget to return things where they got them. For them, of course, it isn't necessary. Passing notes. Even if a blind person can write (I print on about a first grade level), he cannot receive notes, which is half the fun. Dressing in style. Both because to be up to date means to change (change is always difficult) and because comfortable clothes are loose, because you don't know what to do with the sudden curls or the new chain, or which finger wears the ring. Participating in group sports. Roller skating and running are possible with a buddy, and waterskiing is easy, but most sports are impossible, and dancing is tough. Movies are a maybe and soap operas are lots easier to follow on TV than dramas. Cartoons aren't worth the trouble (too much lost in the translation). Singing is okay and blind people can learn to play musical instruments. The problems with swimming are two: bumping into other people and losing one's orientation. Knowing if THEY are talking to YOU. This problem goes both ways. The blind person doesn't know and the sighted person doesn't know if the blind person knows. In restaurants, the waitress often asks my companion "What does she want?", thereby avoiding the problem. Sighted persons do not use names when speaking to people and do not speak when they enter a room. They stand by a blind person and expect to be recognized or ask a direct question to one person in a group and don't realize that the blind won't know to whom the question is addressed. Knowing which floor the elevator stopped on. Although it often possible to guess which button to push to request a given floor, especially if the building is familiar, it is not possible without some kind of cue to determine where the elevator has stopped. I have been stranded in the basement of the building where I work, unable to find the call button. I have also been deposited on floors I cannot identify and have been forced to get back onto the elevator and hope for a better result next try. Although this is usually not dangerous, it is humiliating and certainly a bother. Determining whether this is the elevated/subway train you want. Even if you know which one you want, there is no announcement as to which one you got. Finding the door in the alotted few seconds is also difficult as well as not completely losing your orientation in the unbelievable noise of a subway. I like riding the subway, but the absolute terror of the noise which completely destroys all auditory clues is almost more than I can handle. Finding the bathroom. You don't want to ask and they are embarassed when you do. (Do they think they will be asked to help?) If you do get to the bathroom with their help, they will insist on showing you where the toilet is, but will not hear you ask about the toilet paper. Toilets are big things and are usually in little rooms on the floor, but toilet paper can be anywhere! Going out with the guys. They always have to think of you, to consider your limitations. This leaves you always a bit of a liability even if they really do want you along. Sometimes a kid/person can purchase a place. It's never easy. Crossing streets. Not causing panic like the subway, crossing streets is nevertheless an extremely stressful necessity. You go forward when the traffic besides you goes forward. Sometimes cars go forward prior to doing a right turn on red. Often the up curb is a different height from the down curb. Sometimes one or both curbs is/are not there at all. Unlike sighted people, blind people must not cross against the light. Cars are often silent and oftener swift. Holding one's temper when sighted people take you across the street. I have been pushed across streets I did not want to cross. I have been told, "I will help you" (unasked) and had my cane hand grasped and the cane thereby made useless. Short of being truly rude (and next time I might really need the help), there is nothing to do but try to accept as help what is meant to be help instead of responding to the indignity as it is. Finding a person/colleague. Even if you know the general area the individual frequents, it is difficult to make the initial contact. The blind must either barge in (is Fitz somewhere around here?) or wait for someone to ask if he/she is looking for someone. This may take a long time if all the desks in the room are empty. I know one man who talked to himself in such situations hoping that someone would answer. This behavior often caused more problems than it solved. (Guy must be a nut.) When we can, Pat and I ride home together on the train. We always sit in the same car, the one closest to the crosswalk at our stop.

Because it is so difficult to find each other, we meet in the station. Recently, after working late, I didn't have time to let Pat know I would be riding with him. I got on the usual car, found a seat and listened for the telltale sound blind people make, clicking of a watch, folding of a cane, Pat clearing his throat. I knew he had to be there somewhere, but short of going down the aisle and asking each person if he was the most wonderful guy in the world, I couldn't dream up a way to find him. The conductor came to collect tickets. "Hello Pat and Anna," he said. The gentlemen beside me was Pat. To know what pretty is, for myself. To know what pretty is for someone else. To care. I am glad my daughter is pretty, but it means nothing to me in terms of what kind of person she is or how we relate to each other. I believe that physical beauty is a gift, to be treasured like the sunrise the velvet twilight, or the wild merriment of a calliope. I believe it is wrong when because of physical prettiness a person's stature is increased, and it is a sin when for lack of it one's value is even in a small way diminished. Mobility. Like the sighted traveler in a blizzard, the blind person wishing to move from one place to another is woefully short of information about his surroundings. He may be walking north seeking south, wandering in the proverbial circle or standing perfectly still three feet from his objective. The blind child must learn early to interpret the cues that are available to him; the sidewalk; the traffic, both vehicular and pedestrian; the wind; the sun; the height of the curb; the sharpness of a turn. He needs to know exactly where it is he wants to go (three blocks south, two driveways after the picket fence) and a method of determining whether he has arrived there.

Many blind people use a cane to feel the sidewalk. Some, often those less confident, choose a guide dog. Still others go places only if a sighted person is available to go along. The skills necessary for independent travel are not easily developed. The blind child must learn how to trip but not fall, listen for cars people and bicycles, to get lost and retrace his path exactly until he is back in familiar territory, to put coins in a drop box on a bus, to be always attentive not only to where he is going, but also where he has been. He may not listen to the radio as he goes along as the sound will obscure his clues. In cold weather he must choose a hat and gloves with special care because covering fingers and ears is like covering eyes. When the ground is covered with snow, he must be aware that he is in real danger of becoming seriously disoriented because his feet can no longer discern the landmarks they have come to know. Experience, the more the better, will teach him. Before I went to kindergarten, I walked alone the two blocks to the store. When I was eight, I walked the mile to my girlfriend's house to play. Last month I missed the bus and had to carry my 6-month-old baby safely the two miles to the doctor for her routine checkup. It wasn't fun, but we arrived safely and no one at the office knew there had been a problem. It is important to be self-reliant. The person who arouses another's pity is not, after all, the person who arouses another's respect, and I choose to be respected. The person who is cared for is not the one who is given responsibility, and I choose to be responsible. For the handicapped person as well as the nonhandicapped person, life is a continum of choices, to choose to be pleased with a gift, to choose to do the difficult task, to choose not to be offended. Learning to make the right choices begins in infancy. I will (not?) explore, be cheerful, eat this ugly (pretty?) food, return my daddy's smile, pick myself up when I fall down. The choice that is natural is usually the easy choice instead of the best choice. It is the parent who must make the right choices and accept responsibility for the pain they cause. The demand on parents is especially great when the child is handicapped. Wishing to offer only that which gives joy, they work to spare him not only those hurts his handicap might cause (if you run, you might get hurt) but also those that a normal child would meet (If you roller skate down a curb you might get hurt) robbing him not only of childhood, but of a self-reliant adulthood as well. The good parents never says, "you can't do that because you are blind." He says, "Be careful." My mother tells a story about sending me to the store when I was small and my overhearing someone say to someone else, "Oh, she's a blind poor little thing." Her response was "well, do you feel like a poor little thing?" Because of the wisdom, the insistence, the sense of humor (never underestimate a sense of humor) of my parents, it never occurred to me to be a poor little thing. I pray that it will never occur to my children either.

If the attitude of the public toward the handicapped has changed even a little in my lifetime, I would like to think that I have helped to change it, but changes are often difficult to discern. More than once, as Pat waited for me on the street dressed in a suit, minding his own business, a passer-by has placed money in his hand and disappeared as Pat was trying to refuse it. When I sent a resume to one prospective employer, he chose not to interview me, explaining to an acquaintance of mine that a blind person could not have done the things I said I had done. When I volunteered by phone to chair a committee for the local children's chorus, I was accepted enthusiastically, but when I appeared at the group's general meeting, the chairmanship was assigned to someone else. It is difficult, almost impossible to view oneself as a useful contributing human being when society as a whole is so sure you are inept. You fight the little battles, the cop-out battles constantly (to sew on a button, to pay your bills on time, to jump rope or run or ice skate or ride a bike or win at trivial pursuit or dress like the other guys). But these are small compared to the real battle, the one for self-esteem. Honestly, I am not physically as good as a sighted person. Honestly, my baby is not as potentially safe in my care as the care of someone who can see. I cannot drive my children to parties, choose their clothes, judge the length of their hair, evaluate their handwriting, teach them body language. I can't even go to the grocery store without help. Do I feel sorry for myself? Of course, but defining the problem is the first step toward solving it, and one can use self-pity as an aid to definition. I don't recommend it, but handicapped people aren't saints, they're just people with handicaps, and everyone feels sorry for himself sometimes. Knowing I am inferior and trying to face it with patience and courage is a constant wearying task. I try harder always than the other guy because to appear equal I must be better. I don't usually blame someone/thing else when things go wrong, because when you blame outside sources for a problem, the solution is out of your hands. I count my blessings, often, very often, because they are many.

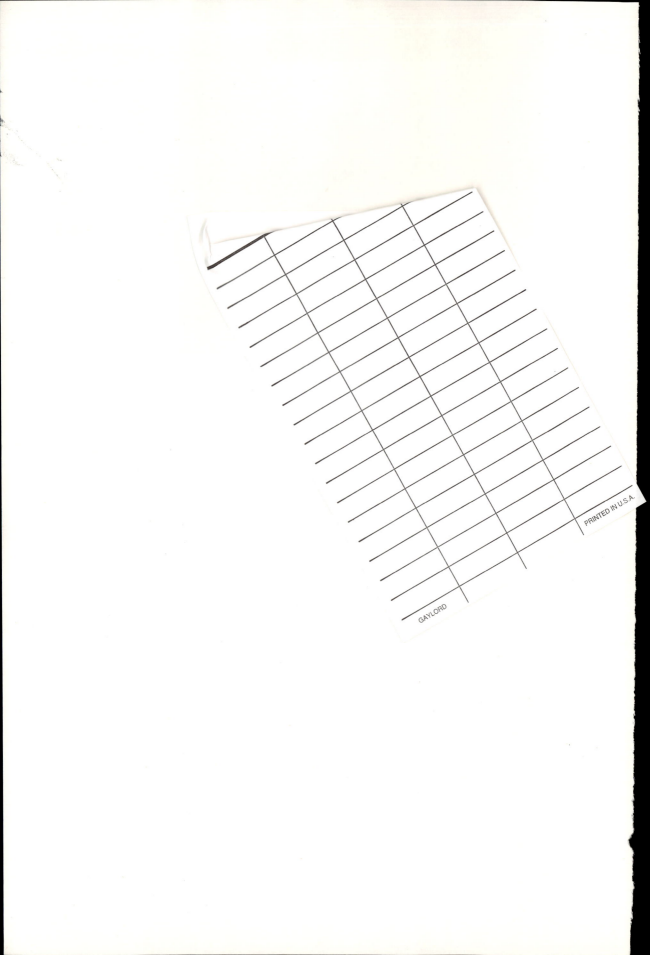

GAYLORD

PRINTED IN U.S.A.